Challenge

Maths

Steve Mills and Hilary Koll

Age 11–14
Years 7–9
Key Stage 3

Introduction

This *Maths Challenge* book will challenge and extend you in key Maths topics in the curriculum at Key Stage 3.

This book is designed to be used throughout the year. Each double-page spread provides information about the nature of the topic, the key aspects that you are expected to master, and provides opportunities for you to practise and test your understanding. You will need to write your answers in a separate notebook.

Throughout the book are 'Try it yourself!' puzzles which encourage you to develop more effective thinking skills. These can be tackled independently of the rest of the page and can serve as a revision question when a topic is revisited.

By working through the *Maths Challenge* book, you will encounter the more difficult Mathematics concepts appropriate for your year group and be encouraged to solve problems and puzzles requiring an advanced level of mathematical thinking.

Hachette UK's policy is to use papers that are natural, renewable and recyclable products and made from wood grown in sustainable forests. The logging and manufacturing processes are expected to conform to the environmental regulations of the country of origin.

Orders: please contact Bookpoint Ltd, 130 Milton Park, Abingdon, Oxon OX14 4SB. Telephone: +44 (0)1235 827720. Fax: +44 (0)1235 400454. Lines are open 9.00a.m.–5.00p.m., Monday to Saturday, with a 24-hour message answering service. Visit our website at www.hoddereducation.co.uk.

© Steve Mills and Hilary Koll 2013
Teacher's tips © Matt Koster 2013
First published in 2007 exclusively for WHSmith by
Hodder Education
An Hachette UK Company
Carmelite House
50 Victoria Embankment
London EC4Y 0DZ

This second edition published in 2013 exclusively for WHSmith.

Impression number   10 9
Year   2021 2020 2019

Cover Illustration by Oxford Designers and Illustrators Ltd
Illustrations © Hodder Education
Typeset in Folio Book 10 on 12pt by DC Graphic Design Ltd, Swanley Village, Kent.
Printed in Spain

A catalogue record for this title is available from the British Library

ISBN 978 1444 189 254

Contents

You will revise:
- writing numbers in standard form.

 Get started

Our number system is based on groups of 10.

Notice how the numbers can be written with powers, such as 10^4 or 10^{-1}. These powers of 10 are used when writing numbers in **standard form**. For example, 3 420 000 is written as 3.42×10^6.

B	HM	TM	M	HTh	TTh	Th	H	T	U	t	h	th		
1	0	0	0	0	0	0	0	0	0				one billion	10^9
	1	0	0	0	0	0	0	0	0				one hundred million	10^8
		1	0	0	0	0	0	0	0				ten million	10^7
			1	0	0	0	0	0	0				one million	10^6
				1	0	0	0	0	0				one hundred thousand	10^5
					1	0	0	0	0				ten thousand	10^4
						1	0	0	0				one thousand	10^3
							1	0	0				one hundred	10^2
								1	0				ten	10^1
									1				one	10^0
									0	1			one tenth	10^{-1}
									0	0	1		one hundredth	10^{-2}
									0	0	0	1	one thousandth	10^{-3}

 **Practice**

1 Multiply these numbers.

    a 34×1000 **b** $65 \times 100\,000$ **c** 22×100

    d $375 \times 1\,000\,000$ **e** $27 \times 10\,000$ **f** 110×0.01

    g 297×0.1 **h** 654×0.001

 Challenge

2 Multiply these numbers.

    a $3.5 \times 100\,000$ **b** $9.4 \times 10\,000$ **c** 6.8×1000

    d 7.43×0.01 **e** 4.2×0.1 **f** 1.95×0.001

3 Multiply these numbers. For example, $3.8 \times 10^4 = 38\,000$.

a 4.7×10^5

b 4.32×10^2

c 9.78×10^6

d 5.5×10^4

e 4.8×10^1

f 7×10^0

g 1.2×10^{-1}

h 8.6×10^{-2}

i 7×10^{-3}

Try it yourself!

Which of these numbers is the largest? Which is the smallest?

9×10^6

9.3×10^{-2}

1.2×10^{-5}

9.1×10^6

4.5×10^7

3×10^{-4}

4 Which of these numbers are correctly written in standard form?

A 3.6×10^6

B 84×10^3

C 97.2×1000

D 7.73×10^4

E $9.8 \div 10^{-3}$

F 2.5×10^9

G 2500

H 32×10

I 8.65×10^{-2}

J $5.4 \div 10^{-3}$

5 Write these numbers in standard form.

a $34\,000\,000$

b $230\,000$

c 7870

d $50\,000$

e $12\,500\,000$

f $23\,400\,000$

g 0.004

h $0.000\,002$

i $0.000\,065$

j $0.003\,28$

6 Which numbers are equivalent to the boxed number?

a $\boxed{48\,000}$

48×10^2

4.8×10^4

48×10^3

$4.8 \times 10\,000$

0.48×10^3

b $\boxed{125\,000}$

$125 \times 10\,000$

125×10^3

1.25×10^5

12.5×1000

1.25×10^4

c $\boxed{0.0042}$

42×10^{-2}

4.2×10^{-4}

4.2×10^{-3}

4.2×0.001

42×10^{-4}

7 In each part of question 6, which correctly shows the number in standard form?

How did I do?

I can write numbers in standard form.

✔ ☐

Teacher's tips

In a power of ten, the exponent (the small number above and to the right of the 10) denotes how many places from the decimal to move the number. Positive exponents to the left, negative exponents to the right.

You will revise:

▶ how to calculate with fractions.

Get started

If fractions have the *same* denominator it is easy to add or subtract them.

▶ Add or subtract the numerators.

▶ Leave denominators the same.

If the fractions do *not* have the same denominator, change them to equivalent fractions that *do* have the same denominator before adding or subtracting.

Multiplying fractions is easy.

▶ Multiply the numerators.

▶ Multiply the denominators.

To make the multiplication easier, change each fraction to its simplest form and try to cancel diagonally (by dividing the numerator of one fraction by the denominator of the other), like this:

$$\frac{\overset{1}{\cancel{5}}}{\underset{7}{\cancel{49}}} \times \frac{\overset{2}{\cancel{14}}}{\underset{3}{\cancel{15}}} = \frac{2}{21}$$

Dividing fractions can be done using multiplication. This makes it much easier. Turn the second fraction in the question upside down and multiply them. You get the same answer!

Practice

1 Answer these questions. The fractions in each pair do NOT have the same denominator. You will need to change one or both fractions to equivalent ones with the same denominator. Write fractions in their simplest form.

a $\frac{3}{20} + \frac{1}{4}$ **b** $\frac{1}{6} + \frac{3}{4}$ **c** $\frac{2}{7} + \frac{1}{3}$ **d** $\frac{2}{5} + \frac{1}{4}$

e $\frac{7}{8} - \frac{1}{6}$ **f** $\frac{4}{5} - \frac{3}{10}$ **g** $\frac{9}{10} - \frac{3}{4}$ **h** $\frac{2}{5} - \frac{1}{8}$

Challenge

2 Answer these questions.

a $\frac{2}{10} + \frac{1}{3} + \frac{2}{5}$ **b** $\frac{1}{8} + \frac{1}{6} + \frac{1}{4}$ **c** $\frac{3}{4} + \frac{2}{7} + \frac{1}{8}$

d $\frac{1}{3} + \frac{4}{5} + \frac{5}{6}$ **e** $\frac{8}{9} - \frac{1}{6}$ **f** $\frac{5}{7} - \frac{1}{10}$

g $\frac{6}{9} - \frac{3}{8}$ **h** $\frac{5}{7} - \frac{1}{6}$

3 Answer these questions. Give each fractional answer in its simplest form.

a $\frac{2}{3} \times \frac{5}{7}$

b $\frac{5}{6} \times \frac{4}{5}$

c $\frac{4}{9} \times \frac{8}{10}$

d $\frac{2}{7} \times \frac{3}{4}$

e $\frac{5}{8} \times \frac{1}{6}$

f $\frac{5}{6} \times \frac{1}{7}$

Try it yourself!

Which of these questions has the greatest answer?

A $\frac{2}{3} - \frac{2}{9}$

B $\frac{4}{5} \times \frac{15}{20}$

C $\frac{7}{10} \div \frac{14}{20}$

D $\frac{3}{8} + \frac{1}{3}$

4 Answer these questions. Give each fractional answer in its simplest form.

a $\frac{3}{4} \div \frac{2}{7}$

b $\frac{2}{9} \div \frac{3}{5}$

c $\frac{4}{7} \div \frac{2}{3}$

d $\frac{7}{8} \div \frac{1}{9}$

e $\frac{4}{5} \div \frac{1}{2}$

f $\frac{7}{10} \div \frac{3}{5}$

g $\frac{6}{7} \div \frac{3}{4}$

h $\frac{5}{9} \div \frac{7}{8}$

5 Answer these questions. Give each fractional answer in its simplest form.

a $\frac{15}{16} \times \frac{24}{25}$

b $\frac{15}{35} \times \frac{7}{20}$

c $\frac{35}{56} \times \frac{8}{15}$

d $\frac{5}{27} \times \frac{18}{55}$

e $\frac{15}{24} \times \frac{16}{30}$

f $\frac{48}{60} \times \frac{15}{42}$

g $\frac{12}{32} \times \frac{16}{36}$

h $\frac{21}{30} \times \frac{6}{28}$

6 Answer these questions. Give each fractional answer in its simplest form.

a $\frac{15}{32} \div \frac{20}{24}$

b $\frac{3}{45} \div \frac{9}{15}$

c $\frac{35}{72} \div \frac{25}{24}$

d $\frac{45}{42} \div \frac{6}{7}$

e $\frac{33}{36} \div \frac{11}{18}$

f $\frac{45}{12} \div \frac{35}{18}$

g $\frac{7}{16} \div \frac{11}{44}$

h $\frac{7}{27} \div \frac{35}{45}$

How did I do?

I can add, subtract, multiply and divide fractions. ✔ ☐

Teacher's tips

A quick way to make two fractions equivalent is to multiply both parts of the first fraction by the denominator of the second, then multiply both parts of the second fraction by the (original) denominator of the first. Both answers should then be simplified.

3: Percentages (1)

Get started

A **percentage** is a fraction with a denominator of 100, but written in a different way.

'Per cent' means 'out of a hundred'. 36% means $\frac{36}{100}$.

To work out percentages in your head it can help to find these percentages first:

To find **50%**: halve the number.

To find **25%**: halve the number and halve the answer (or divide by 4).

To find **10%**: divide the number by 10.

To find **1%**: divide the number by 100.

Practice

1 Copy and complete these.

a 50% of   =
25% of   **240**   =
10% of   =
1% of   =

b 50% of   =
25% of   **160**   =
10% of   =
1% of   =

2 Work these out.

a 50% of £28   **b** 50% of 36 m   **c** 25% of £88

d 25% of 600 g   **e** 10% of 530 cm   **f** 10% of 25 m

Challenge

3 Copy and complete these.

a 75% of   =
30% of   **240**   =
5% of   =
2% of   =

b 30% of   =
2% of   **160**   =
15% of   =
60% of   =

4 Answer these. Remember to write the unit of measurement each time.

a 30% of £120   **b** 2% of 300 m   **c** 5% of £80

d 2% of 500 kg   **e** 90% of 60 cm   **f** 60% of 110 m

g 70% of 90 mm   **h** 5% of 360 cm   **i** 95% of 20 cm

5 Work these out without a calculator.

a In a sale you pay 70% of the original price. The original price for a shirt is £30. How much is the sale price?

b A woman who earns £24 000 in a year gives 5% of her earnings to charity. How much does she give each year?

c A baby girl weighs 90% of her expected weight. Her expected weight was 110 ounces. How much does she weigh?

6 **a** Find these percentages.

| 50% of 360 |
| 25% of 360 |
| 10% of 360 |
| 5% of 360 |
| 1% of 360 |
| $\frac{1}{2}$% of 360 |

b Now use your answers to find these.

60% of 360	51% of 360
75% of 360	35% of 360
15% of 360	50.5% of 360
$25\frac{1}{2}$% of 360	16% of 360
11% of 360	66% of 360
6% of 360	$15\frac{1}{2}$% of 360

7 A worker is paid £55 a week day. If he works at the weekend he is paid 11% extra. How much does he earn if he works 7 days a week for:

a one week?   **b** two weeks?   **c** four weeks?

8 10% of £250 has an answer that is a whole number of pounds, £25.

a Which of these is a whole number of pounds?

1% of £250	2% of £250	3% of 250
4% of 250	5% of 250	6% of 250

How did I do?

b For £250, can you find a rule or rules that will tell you which percentages give whole-number answers?

I can calculate percentages of quantities. ✔ ☐

Teacher's tips

The trick to mentally solving percentages is to break the question into easier parts. So 70% is found by finding 10% then multiplying by 7, 15% is 10% plus 5% (half of 10%), and so on. Practise 'chunking' problems this way.

4: Percentages (2)

You will revise:

▶ how to use percentage changes to solve problems.

Get started

To **increase** by a percentage	To **decrease** by a percentage
▶ Find the percentage of the amount. ▶ Add this on to the original amount. Increase £146 by 32%. 32% of 146 is 46.72. £146 + £46.72 = £192.72	▶ Find the percentage of the amount. ▶ Subtract this from the original amount. Decrease £146 by 32% 32% of 146 is 46.72. £146 − £46.72 = £99.28

If a question gives the *new* price of something after a percentage change, you can find the *original* price.

In a sale, prices are reduced by 28%. A jacket costs £42.84 in the sale. What was its original price?

Original price	Percentage change	Sale price	Sale price as % of original price
?	28% decrease	£42.84	72%

▶ Write the sale price and new percentage:

£42.84 is 72%.

▶ Divide the sale price to find 1%:

£42.84 ÷ 72 = 0.595 is 1%

▶ Multiply by 100 to find 100%:

0.595 × 100 = 59.50 is 100%

Original price £59.50

Practice

1 Answer these percentage questions using a calculator. Remember to write the unit of measurement each time.

    a 47% of £40   **b** 33% of £22   **c** 57% of £58

    d 44.5% of 26 kg   **e** 17.5% of 38 kg   **f** 15% of 144 kg

    g 9% of 53 ml   **h** 3% of 125 m   **i** 4.5% of 306 ml

Challenge

2 A house was worth £170 000 in 2000. By the year 2004 its value had increased by 78%. What was the value of the house in 2004?

3 A man weighed 96 kg. His weight decreased by 17%. How much does he weigh now?

4 Answer these percentage-change questions. Use a calculator.

a Increase 72 m by 34%.

b Increase £125 000 by 53%.

c Increase 29.5 km by 4%.

d Decrease 940 g by 37%.

e Decrease £13 400 by 17.5%.

f Decrease 45.8 kg by 9%.

g Increase 900 ml by 94%.

h Increase 67 cm by 12.6%.

i Increase 48 mm by 3.2%.

j Decrease £92 by 6.5%.

k Decrease 13.27 kg by 58%.

l Decrease 190 m by 9.9%.

5 Copy and complete this percentage-change table. The first row is done for you.

Original price	Percentage change	Amount to be increased/decreased by	New price	New price as percentage of original price
£53	17% increase	£9.01	£62.01	100% + 17% = 117%
£950	8% decrease			100% − 8% = 92%
£265	63% increase			
£1200	36% decrease			
£45 000	81% increase			
£290 000	29% decrease			

6 Answer these percentage-change questions. Use a calculator.

a In a sale, prices are reduced by 54%. A jacket costs £26.68 in the sale. What was its original price?

b In the New Year, prices rise by 7%. A skirt costs £39.59 after the rise. What was its original price?

c In the New Year, prices rise by 12.5%. A hat costs £31.50 after the rise. What was its original price?

d A car is being driven along a road. It decreases its speed by 22% to reach a speed of 31.2 mph. At what speed was it travelling before it slowed down?

e A man's weight goes up by 14% to 89.604 kg. How much did he weigh before the increase?

How did I do?

I can use percentage changes to solve problems. ✔ ☐

Teacher's tips

Remember, the original number is always 100%, whatever its value. All increases or decreases are related to that original (100%) value. A 10% increase is 110% of the original; a 10% decrease is 90% of the original.

5: Direct proportion

You will revise:
- direct proportion
- how to use the unitary method to solve problems involving direct proportion.

Get started

When a quantity gets larger or smaller, it is said to change. Sometimes a change in one quantity causes a change, or is linked to a change, in another quantity. If these changes happen in the same ratio, then the quantities are said to be in **direct proportion**.

Direct proportion problems can be solved using the **unitary method**.

- Divide to find 'one'.
- Then multiply to find 'many'.

£11 is worth the same as 17.38 euros. How many euros is £48?
- Divide 17.38 by 11 to find how many euros is the same as 'one' pound:
  17.38 ÷ 11 = 1.58
- Then multiply 1.58 by 48 to find how much £48 is in euros:
  1.58 × 48 = 75.84 euros

Practice

1 These tables show quantities in direct proportion. Copy and complete them.

a

1	7
2	14
8	
100	

b

3	24
5	40
7	
20	

c

6	4.5
9	6.75
11	
15	

Challenge

2 Answer these direct proportion questions. You may use a calculator.

a Seven portions of chips cost £26.18. How much will three cost?

b Four pasties cost £3.48. How much will three cost?

c Six onion bhajis cost £7.02. How much will five cost?

d Two prawn kormas cost £13.84. How much will five cost?

e Eight ribs cost £7.76. How much will three cost?

f Four cheese slices cost £5.48. How much will three cost?

3 Each table shows quantities in direct proportion. For each table, write an equation showing the relationship between the quantities.

a

No. of kebabs (n)	Cost (c)
1	£2.25
2	£4.50
8	£18
100	£225

b

No. of burgers (n)	Cost (c)
2	£7
3	£10.50
7	£24.50
20	£70

c

No. of hot dogs (n)	Cost (c)
7	£12.25
9	£15.75
11	£19.25
85	£148.75

4 Which of these show pairs that are directly proportional to each other?

A The circumference (C) of a circle and its diameter (d).

B The perimeter (P) of a regular hexagon and the length (l) of one of its sides.

C The area (A) of a circle and the radius squared (r^2).

D The area (A) of a square and the length of a side squared (l^2).

E The distance (D) a cyclist travels and the number of revolutions (R) of the wheel of the bicycle.

F The cost (c) of tickets for a concert and the number (n) of tickets purchased.

G The perimeter (P) of a square and the length (l) of one of its sides.

5 For parts **a** to **d** in question 4, write an equation to describe the relationships between the two quantities.

6 Four different types of cereal bars contain nuts and oats. Which of these bars has the highest ratio of nuts to oats?

Bar A: 450 g nuts, 250 g oats

Bar B: 300 g nuts, 160 g oats

Bar C: 800 g nuts, 680 g oats

Bar D: 73 g nuts, 41 g oats

How did I do?

I can recognise when two quantities are directly proportional. ☐

I can use the unitary method to solve direct proportion problems. ☐

Teacher's tips

'Find one, find many' – if you start by calculating the value of one, then finding the value of many is easy. When using a calculator, check if the answer looks right – it's easy to mistype and get a wrong answer.

6: Ratio

You will revise:
- dividing an amount in a given ratio
- simplifying and comparing ratios.

Get started

Ratio gives the relationship between two or more numbers or quantities. It compares 'part with part'.

To divide an amount in a given ratio:

- find out how many parts there are in the ratio altogether
- divide the amount to find what 'one' part is worth
- multiply to find 'many' parts.

When a ratio includes a fraction or a decimal, rewrite it into the simplest whole-number form. Multiply the numbers in the ratio by the same number to make them both whole numbers, like this:

Sometimes it can be difficult to compare two ratios, so the ratios are changed to the form $1 : m$ or $m : 1$, where m is a decimal. Use a calculator to divide one number in the ratio by the other.

Practice

1 Answer these ratio questions. You may use a calculator.

    a Divide £2.38 in the ratio 3 : 4.

    b Divide £18.81 in the ratio 8 : 1.

    c Divide £30.48 in the ratio 1 : 3 : 4.

Challenge

2 Write each ratio in its simplest whole-number form.

    a 3.5 : 2   **b** $\frac{1}{2}$: 3   **c** 3 : 0.2   **d** $\frac{1}{4}$: $6\frac{1}{2}$

    e 3 : 2.4   **f** 0.75 : 4   **g** 2 : $\frac{1}{4}$: $\frac{1}{2}$ **h** 1.2 : 2 : 3

3 Change each ratio to the form 1 : m, by dividing the second number in the ratio by the first. Use a calculator. Round your answers to two decimal places.

a 2 : 9	b 5 : 9	c 8 : 17	d 7 : 11

e 15 : 25	f 4.5 : 7	g 16 : 13	h 0.8 : 42

4 A pound coin is made from copper, zinc and nickel in the ratio 140 : 49 : 11. The coin weighs 9.5 g. How many grams of copper, zinc and nickel are used to make one coin?

5 Here are some ratios about the performance of several tennis players in a tournament. The ratio of aces served to double faults is given for each player and the ratio of games won to games lost.

Player	aces : double faults	games won : games lost
Sandy Hurry	50 : 40	31 : 18
Roger Fedwell	24 : 12	64 : 12
Maria Handitova	2 : 16	40 : 63
Vera Williamson	33 : 66	57 : 28
Justine Winnin	14 : 49	15 : 18

a Copy the table, writing all the ratios in the form 1 : m and rounding the ratios to two decimal places.

b Which player had the best ratio of aces to double faults?

c Which player had the best ratio of games won to games lost?

6 Four T-shirts are made from polyester (P) and cotton (C). Change each ratio to the form 1 : m.

T-shirt A   P : C = 2.4 : 6

T-shirt B   P : C = 5 : 7

T-shirt C   P : C = 3.5 : 2

T-shirt D   P : C = 5 : 7.75

Which T-shirt has the highest ratio of cotton?

How did I do?

I can divide an amount in a given ratio. ☐

I can simplify ratios. ☐

I can compare ratios by writing them in the form 1 : m or m : 1. ☐

Teacher's tips

When simplifying ratios, remember you must always do the same thing to all the parts.

When dividing in a ratio, first find the unit part. E.g. divide 90 in the ratio 2:3:4. Let 'a' be the unit part, so 2a + 3a + 4a = 90, so 9a = 90, so a = 10 therefore the answer is 20:30:40.

7: Positive and negative numbers

You will revise:
▶ how to add and subtract positive and negative numbers.

Get started

Positive and negative numbers can be shown on a number line.

$$-10\ -9\ -8\ -7\ -6\ -5\ -4\ -3\ -2\ -1\ \ 0\ \ 1\ \ 2\ \ 3\ \ 4\ \ 5\ \ 6\ \ 7\ \ 8\ \ 9\ \ 10$$

negative numbers   positive numbers

When *adding* numbers, count along the number line towards the *right*.

When *subtracting* numbers, count along the number line towards the *left*.

When two signs appear next to each other:

▶ think of $-\ -$ as a $+$, so $1 - -3 = 1 + 3$
▶ think of $+\ -$ as a $-$, so $-3 + -4 = -3 - 4$.

Practice

1 Work out these additions, moving to the right on the number line.

    a $-6 + 9$ **b** $-9 + 4$ **c** $-3 + 7$

    d $-4 + 9$ **e** $-2 + 6$

2 Work out these subtractions, moving to the left on the number line.

    a $-2 - 3$ **b** $5 - 8$ **c** $-4 - 8$

    d $0 - 7$ **e** $-4 - 5$

Challenge

3 Work these out.

    a $-5 + 9 =$ **b** $-7 - 2 =$ **c** $11 - 15 =$

       $-5 - 9 =$ $7 - 2 =$ $-11 - 15 =$

       $5 - 9 =$ $-7 + 2 =$ $-11 + 15 =$

4 Work these out.

    a $-21 + 9$ **b** $-15 + 4$ **c** $-13 + 20$ **d** $-27 + 13$

    e $-12 + 16$ **f** $-12 - 13$ **g** $21 - 28$ **h** $-24 - 8$

    i $0 - 17$ **j** $-40 - 5$

5 Change each question to make it easier to answer, then answer it.
For example, $2 - -8 = 2 + 8 = 10$

a $-6 - -4$ b $-5 + -8$ c $5 + -9$ d $3 - -5$

e $-9 + -3$ f $15 - -11$ g $17 + -5$ h $-18 + -4$

6 In a quiz show, contestants score 2 points for a correct answer,
-3 points for an incorrect answer and -1 point for a question not
answered. What did each contestant score in total?

a not answered, correct, correct, incorrect, incorrect, correct,
not answered

b correct, incorrect, correct, incorrect, correct, not answered,
incorrect

c not answered, incorrect, correct, incorrect, correct, not answered,
correct

d correct, correct, not answered, incorrect, incorrect, incorrect,
correct, not answered

7 Here are five number cards.

| -6 | | -9 | | 8 | | 4 | | -11 |

Which cards can be used to make each statement correct? Copy and
complete them.

a $\square + \square = -2$

c $\square - \square = -2$

b $\square + \square = 2$

d $\square - \square = 2$

8 Copy and complete these magic squares so that each row, column
and diagonal has the total shown.

a Total: 3

b Total: -3

Try it yourself!

Copy and complete this magic
square so that each row, column
and diagonal has the total -9.

		0
	-3	-7
-6		

How did I do?

I can add and subtract positive
and negative numbers.

Teacher's tips

A double negative is a positive; subtracting a negative number is equivalent to adding it
(just like saying "I don't not like chips" means "I like chips"). When using the number line
don't miss out zero – a common mistake is to jump from -1 straight to 1.

You will revise:
▶ integer arithmetic.

Get started

The set of **integers** is the set of positive and negative whole numbers and zero. These are all integers: 5, 125, 4, −6, 0, −27, 36, −100.

When multiplying and dividing integers, use this table to help you decide what sign the answer should have.

positive × positive = positive 3 × 5 = 15	positive ÷ positive = positive 15 ÷ 5 = 3
positive × negative = negative 3 × −5 = −15	positive ÷ negative = negative 15 ÷ −5 = −3
negative × positive = negative −3 × 5 = −15	negative ÷ positive = negative −15 ÷ 5 = −3
negative × negative = positive −3 × −5 = 15	negative ÷ negative = positive −15 ÷ −5 = 3

Because two negatives make a positive, when a negative number is squared the answer is positive:

$$7^2 = 7 \times 7 = 49 \qquad\qquad (-7)^2 = -7 \times -7 = 49$$

This means that there are two solutions to $\sqrt{49}$. One answer is 7, the other −7. To show both solutions the $\pm$ sign is used: $\sqrt{49} = \pm 7$.

Practice

1 Work these out in your head. Write down the answers.

    a −3 × −10   **b** −6 × 5   **c** −70 ÷ 10   **d** −25 ÷ −5

    e 8 × −10   **f** −3 × −8   **g** −24 ÷ −4   **h** 32 ÷ −4

Challenge

2 Answer these multiplication and division questions.

    a −7 × −8   **b** −10 × 9   **c** −48 ÷ 6   **d** −42 ÷ −7

    e 8 × −5   **f** −6 × −9   **g** −32 ÷ −4   **h** 72 ÷ −8

    i −6 × −6   **j** 8 × −6   **k** −81 ÷ −9   **l** −64 ÷ 8

3 Write the value of each of these.

a $(-5)^2$ b $(-3)^2$ c $(-7)^2$ d $(-10)^2$

e $(-9)^2$ f $(-4)^2$ g $(-8)^2$ h $(-6)^2$

4 Find the square root of these numbers, writing the answers with the $\pm$ sign.

a $\sqrt{16}$ b $\sqrt{4}$ c $\sqrt{81}$ d $\sqrt{64}$

e $\sqrt{121}$ f $\sqrt{49}$ g $\sqrt{36}$ h $\sqrt{144}$

5 Copy and complete these tables.

a

p	3	-3	3	-3	7	-7	-7	7
q	8	8	-8	-8	-8	-8	8	8
$p \times q$								

b

p	56	-56	56	-56	-56	56	-56	56
q	7	-7	-7	7	-8	-8	8	8
$p \div q$								

c

p	-90	-12	-60	-11	-70	-80	-30	-50
p^2								

6 Use these numbers: $-6, 8, -4, 4, 3, 12, -8, -2$.

a Pick two of the numbers and find the product. Write three different questions that produce the answer -24.

b Write two different questions that produce the answer 48.

c Write two different questions that produce the answer -48.

d Pick three of the numbers and multiply them. Write four different questions that produce the answer -96.

How did I do?

I can multiply and divide positive and negative numbers.

Teacher's tips

The easy way to remember if an answer should be positive or negative is that the answer is only negative when an odd number of the integers are negative. At all other times the answer is positive (because a double negative is a positive!).

You will revise:

- multiples, including common multiples
- factors, including common factors
- prime numbers.

 Get started

A **multiple** is a number that is in a times table or beyond. For example, multiples of 5 are 5, 10, 15, 20, 25, 30, . . . and carry on, such as 85, 115, 500 etc.

A number is a **common multiple** if it is a multiple of more than one number. For example, 21 is a common multiple of 3 and 7.

Factors are whole numbers that divide exactly into another number without a remainder. For example, the factors of 12 are 1, 2, 3, 4, 6 and 12 as they are the only whole numbers that divide exactly into 12 without a remainder.

A number is a **common factor** if it is a factor of more than one number. For example, 7 is a common factor of 14 and 21.

Prime numbers are whole numbers that have two factors, the number itself and 1. Examples are 2, 3, 5, 7, 11, 13, 17, 19, 23, 29, . . .

To find whether a number is a prime number, see how many factors it has. If it has exactly two factors, then it is prime. This means that the number 1 is not prime because it doesn't have two factors; its only factor is 1.

 Practice

1 Copy and complete this multiplication grid.

×	1	2	3	4	5	6	7	8	9	10	11	12
3							21					
4												
5	5	10	15									
6												
7		14										
8												
9												

Challenge

2 Use your answers to the practice question to help you find the lowest common multiple of:

a 4 and 6   **b** 3 and 7   **c** 7 and 8   **d** 6 and 9

e 5 and 8   **f** 3, 6 and 9   **g** 3, 4 and 9   **h** 5, 4 and 6

3 Find all the factors of:

a 20   **b** 16   **c** 25   **d** 30   **e** 14

f 27   **g** 17   **h** 35   **i** 36   **j** 32

4 Which number in question 3 is prime?

5 Find four numbers between 10 and 30 that have exactly six factors.

6 Use your answers to question 3 to help you find the highest common factor of:

a 14 and 35   **b** 32 and 36   **c** 27 and 17

d 20 and 30   **e** 16 and 32   **f** 25 and 30

g 36 and 30   **h** 14 and 20   **i** 27 and 30

7 Find four numbers between 0 and 30 that have an odd number of factors. What is special about these numbers?

8 Here are some square numbers: 4, 9, 16, 25, 36, 49, 64, 81, 100.

Write each of these square numbers as the sum of two prime numbers. For example, 4 = 2 + 2 (2 is prime).

a 9   **b** 16   **c** 25   **d** 36

e 49   **f** 64   **g** 81   **h** 100

9 Find out which number between 0 and 100 has:

a the fewest factors

b the most factors

c exactly 12 factors.

How did I do?

	✔
I can find multiples and factors of a number.	☐
I can find common multiples and common factors of two numbers.	☐
I can recognise prime numbers.	☐

Teacher's tips

A number can have many factors, especially if it's big and/or it's an even number, so if you're asked to find all the factors don't stop after two or three answers! Remember that the number itself, and 1, are always factors.

10: Prime numbers

Get started

Prime numbers are whole numbers that have two factors, the number itself and 1. Examples are 2, 3, 5, 7, 11, 13, 17, 19, 23, 29, . . .

The number 1 is not prime because it doesn't have two factors; its only factor is 1.

The **prime factor decomposition** of a number is when it is written as the product of its prime factors. Examples are $70 = 2 \times 5 \times 7$, $96 = 2^5 \times 3$, $60 = 2^2 \times 3 \times 5$.

The **highest common factor** (HCF) of two numbers is found using the prime factors that appear in the prime factor decompositions of *both* numbers.

The HCF of 96 and 60 is $2^2 \times 3 = 12$.
12 is the highest factor that divides into 96 and 60.

The **lowest common multiple** (LCM) of two numbers is the set of factors that include both decompositions.

The LCM of 96 and 60 is $2^5 \times 3 \times 5 = 480$.
480 is the lowest multiple of both 96 and 60.

Practice

1 Use these factor trees to find the prime factor decomposition of each number.

a 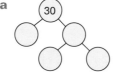 b 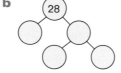 c 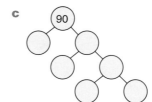 d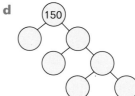

Challenge

2 Draw your own factor trees and find the prime factor decomposition for each of these numbers. Write each prime factor decomposition using powers.

a 16   b 144   c 200

d 135   e 180   f 63

g 120   h 76   i 512

j 343   k 125   l 175

Try it yourself!

Find how many numbers between 1 and 200 have only the prime factor:

a 2

b 3

c 5

3 The prime decompositions of 56 and 64 are shown below.

$$56 = 2^3 \times 7 \qquad\qquad 64 = 2^6$$

a Find the highest common factor (HCF) of 56 and 64.

b Find the lowest common multiple (LCM) of 56 and 64.

4 The prime decompositions of 144 and 216 are shown below.

$$144 = 2^4 \times 3^2 \qquad\qquad 216 = 2^3 \times 3^3$$

a Find the highest common factor (HCF) of 144 and 216.

b Find the lowest common multiple (LCM) of 144 and 216.

5 The prime decompositions of 450 and 756 are shown below.

$$450 = 2 \times 3^2 \times 5^2 \qquad\qquad 756 = 2^2 \times 3^3 \times 7$$

a Find the highest common factor (HCF) of 450 and 756.

b Find the lowest common multiple (LCM) of 450 and 756.

6 Find the prime decompositions of 28 and 48. Use them to help you answer these questions.

a Find the highest common factor (HCF) of 28 and 48.

b Find the lowest common multiple (LCM) of 28 and 48.

7 Find the prime factor decompositions of 84 and 88. Use them to help you to answer these questions.

a Find the highest common factor (HCF) of 84 and 88.

b Find the lowest common multiple (LCM) of 84 and 88.

How did I do?

I can find prime factor decompositions of numbers. □

I can use these to find the HCF and LCM of two numbers. □

You will revise:
- ▶ finding square and cube numbers, and corresponding roots
- ▶ using index notation.

Get started

Square numbers are created by **squaring** a number (multiplying a number by itself).

2^2 (2 squared) $= 2 \times 2 = 4$ $(-2)^2 = -2 \times -2 = 4$
3^2 (3 squared) $= 3 \times 3 = 9$ $(-3)^2 = -3 \times -3 = 9$

Finding the **square root** is the opposite of squaring. The number being multiplied by itself is found.

$\sqrt{4}$ (the square root of 4) $= \pm 2$
$\sqrt{9}$ (the square root of 9) $= \pm 3$

Cubic numbers are created by **cubing** a number:

2^3 (2 cubed) $= 2 \times 2 \times 2 = 8$
3^3 (3 cubed) $= 3 \times 3 \times 3 = 27$

Finding the **cube root** is the opposite of cubing. Cube roots are written using the $\sqrt[3]{}$ sign.

$\sqrt[3]{8}$ (the cube root of 8) $= 2$
$\sqrt[3]{27}$ (the cube root of 27) $= 3$

Practice

1   Write the value of each of these.

    a 5^2 **b** 6^2 **c** 3^2 **d** 7^2 **e** 10^2

    f 2^2 **g** 8^2 **h** 9^2 **i** 12^2 **j** 11^2

Challenge

2   Write the value of each of these cubic numbers.

    a 2^3 **b** 1^3 **c** 3^3 **d** 4^3 **e** 10^3

3   Write these values, remembering to use the $\pm$ sign for square-root questions.

    a $(-5)^2$ **b** $\sqrt{49}$ **c** $\sqrt{81}$ **d** $(-6)^2$ **e** $(-10)^2$

    f $(-11)^2$ **g** $\sqrt{16}$ **h** $(-8)^2$ **i** $\sqrt{100}$ **j** $(-12)^2$

Teacher's tips

Some scientific calculators have function buttons for cubed and squared, but on most calculators you will need to do repeated multiplication. Remember to solve complex expressions using BODMAS – even most scientific calculators won't recognise brackets.

4 Use a calculator to find the value of each of these.

  a $(-15)^2$ **b** $\sqrt{289}$ **c** 32^2 **d** $\sqrt{484}$ **e** $(-19)^2$

  f 8^3 **g** $\sqrt[3]{216}$ **h** $\sqrt[3]{729}$ **i** 11^3 **j** 12^3

5 Use your calculator to help you mark Sandeep's work. If there is a mistake, correct it.

  a $\sqrt{529} = \pm 23$ **b** $44^2 = 1936$

  c $\sqrt[3]{4096} = 16$ **d** $125^3 = 5$

  e $(0.01)^2 = 0.01$ **f** $\sqrt{3375} = 15$

  g $\sqrt[3]{35.739} = 3.3$ **h** $82^3 = 551\,368$

6 Work out the value of each expression.

  a $(4 \times 3)^2$ **b** $(5 + 1)^3$

  c $(5.5)^2$ **d** $(2 \times 4)^3$

  e $\sqrt{4096}$ **f** $\sqrt[3]{9261}$

  g $(-14)^2$ **h** $9^2 + 9^2$

  i $\sqrt{(3^2 + 4^2)}$ **j** $\sqrt{(6^2 + 8^2)}$

  k $4^3 - 8^2$ **l** $(17 - 9)^3$

  m $(2 \times 6)^2$ **n** $(2.5 \times 2)^2$

  o $(5 \times 4)^2$ **p** $\sqrt[3]{2197}$

  q $\sqrt{(5^2 + 12^2)}$ **r** $(5 + 9)^2$

  s $\sqrt{26\,244}$ **t** 6^3

7 Copy and complete these to make the statements true. Each box stands for a missing digit. You may use a calculator.

  a $(\square 7)^2 = \square 2 \square$ **b** $(3\square)^2 = \square\square 1$

  c $(\square 9)^2 = \square 4 \square 1$ **d** $(\square 7)^2 = \square 9 \square\square$

  e $(\square)^3 = \square 1 \square$ **f** $(\square\square)^3 = 9\square\square\square$

  g $(\square\square)^3 = \square\square\square 5$ **h** $(\square\square)^3 = \square 5 \square\square\square$

  i $(\square 5 + 4\square)^3 = \square\square\square 509$

12: Index notation

Get started

When **multiplying** numbers or letters written in index notation you can add the powers, but only if the numbers or letters are the same. This is known as the **index law of multiplication**.

$$8^3 \times 8^2 = (8 \times 8 \times 8) \times (8 \times 8) = 8 \times 8 \times 8 \times 8 \times 8 = 8^5$$

$$8^3 \times 8^2 = 8^{(3+2)} = 8^5$$

When **dividing** numbers or letters written in index notation you can subtract the powers, but only if the numbers or letters are the same. This is known as the **index law of division**.

$$7^5 \div 7^2 = \frac{7 \times 7 \times 7 \times \cancel{7} \times \cancel{7}}{\cancel{7} \times \cancel{7}} = 7^3$$
$$7^5 \div 7^2 = 7^{(5-2)} = 7^3$$

Sometimes when subtracting powers the index is a negative number, like this.

$$7^2 \div 7^5 = \frac{\cancel{7} \times \cancel{7}}{7 \times 7 \times 7 \times \cancel{7} \times \cancel{7}} = 7^{-3}$$
$$7^2 \div 7^5 = 7^{(2-5)} = 7^{-3}$$

The negative sign in a power tells you that it is a fraction with the numerator 1, like these.

$$7^{-3} = \frac{1}{7^3} \qquad 4^{-2} = \frac{1}{4^2} \qquad 3^{-5} = \frac{1}{3^5} \qquad 2^{-1} = \frac{1}{2}$$

Practice

1 Write each of these as a multiplication without any powers. For example, $4^2 = 4 \times 4$.

  a 5^3 b 6^6 c 3^5 d 7^4 e 10^3

  f 2^7 g n^4 h a^5 i p^8

Challenge

2 Write the answers to these in index notation.

  a $6^3 \times 6^2$ b $2^2 \times 2^5$ c $5^4 \times 5^3$ d $10^7 \times 10^7$

  e $8^6 \times 8^2$ f $6^4 \times 6^1$ g $3^7 \times 3^3$ h $4^{10} \times 4^6$

i $n^3 \times n^2$ **j** $a^7 \times a^5$ **k** $x^2 \times x^3$ **l** $y^9 \times y^2$

m $f^6 \times f^4$ **n** $g^4 \times g^0$ **o** $d^1 \times d^4$ **p** $m^3 \times m^3$

3 Write the answers to these in index notation.

a $7^{10} \div 7^5$ **b** $4^8 \div 4^2$ **c** $2^6 \div 2^2$

d $8^6 \div 8^3$ **e** $6^7 \div 6^5$ **f** $9^7 \div 9^6$

g $a^6 \div a^2$ **h** $y^9 \div y^5$ **i** $p^8 \div p^6$

j $s^7 \div s^3$ **k** $m^4 \div m^3$ **l** $w^{12} \div w^{10}$

m $\dfrac{5^5}{5^3}$ **n** $\dfrac{9^{10}}{9^5}$ **o** $\dfrac{7^8}{7^5}$

p $\dfrac{a^8}{a^2}$ **q** $\dfrac{m^{11}}{m^8}$ **r** $\dfrac{y^7}{y^5}$

4 Write the answer to each of these in two different ways.
For example, $7^3 \div 7^7 = 7^{-4} = \dfrac{1}{7^4}$.

a $3^3 \div 3^5$ **b** $2^3 \div 2^9$ **c** $8^4 \div 8^8$

d $\dfrac{m^2}{m^9}$ **e** $\dfrac{p^1}{p^6}$ **f** $\dfrac{k^5}{k^9}$

5 Write the value of each of these without using powers.
For example, $3^{-2} = \dfrac{1}{9}$.

a 2^{-2} **b** 4^2 **c** 4^{-2} **d** 3^{-1}

e 5^{-2} **f** 6^{-2} **g** 10^{-3} **h** 7^{-1}

i 2^4 **j** 2^{-4} **k** 2^{-5} **l** 15^{-1}

Try it yourself!

When two numbers have a product of 1, they are called **reciprocals** of one another. For example, $\frac{1}{4}$ is the reciprocal of 4, since $\frac{1}{4} \times 4 = 1$.

Write the reciprocal of 5 using powers.

How did I do?

I can use index notation (including negative indices) and the index laws.

Teacher's tips

It can be easy to multiply or divide the indices by mistake, when they should be added (for multiplication) or subtracted (for division) – don't get caught out! In algebraic expressions, writing powers longhand will simply look like this $a^4 = a \times a \times a \times a$.

13: Understanding number

You will revise:
- ▶ the order of operations when calculating.

Get started

There are four main **operations** in mathematics: adding, subtracting, multiplying and dividing.

Some questions involve more than one operation. Mathematicians have agreed on an order for doing calculations. The letters of **BODMAS** help you to remember the order of operations.

Do anything in **brackets** first.
Next do **other** things such as squares, roots and powers.
Divide and **multiply** next.

Finally **add** and **subtract**.

Brackets
Other
Divide
Multiply
Add
Subtract

Practice

1 Without using a calculator copy and complete these.

a $36 \times \square = 0$ b $36 \times \square = 36$ c $36 + \square = 36$

d $\square \times 47 = 47$ e $47 - \square = 47$ f $47 \times \square = 0$

g $58 \div \square = 1$ h $58 \times \square = 0$ i $58 \div \square = 58$

j $\square + 95 = 95$ k $\square \times 95 = 95$ l $\square \div 95 = 0$

Challenge

2 Say whether each statement below is true or false.

a Adding zero to a number always gives the answer zero.

b Subtracting zero from a number always gives the number itself.

c Subtraction is the inverse (opposite) of addition.

d Division is the inverse of subtraction.

e Multiplication is the inverse of division.

f It doesn't matter which order you use to add numbers. The answer will always be the same.

Try it yourself!

Rearrange these cards to make questions with these answers. You do not need to use all the cards each time.

a 34   b 16

c 40   d 48

3 Work these out. Remember to use the order of BODMAS.

a $3 + 5 \times 6$

b $(6 + 9) \times 2$

c $16 \div 4 + 4$

d $20 - 16 \div 2$

e $21 \div 3 + 6$

f $14 \div (9 - 2)$

g $5 \times (4 - 2)$

h $(5 + 1)^2$

i $3 \times \sqrt{25}$

j $4 \times 2 + 5$

k $14 - 8 \div 2$

l $(15 - 6) \div 3$

m $(3 + 4) \times 5 + 1$

n $(4 + 6) \times (15 - 12)$

o $3 + 4^2$

4 Which of these have an answer of 16?

A $8 + 4 \times 2$

B $5 + 3 \times 2 + 5$

C $36 \div (2 + 2)$

D $8 + 8 \div 2 - 1$

E $20 - (8 - 4)$

F $\dfrac{6 \times 8}{6 - 3}$

5 A calculator has a broken key. The multiplication key $\times$ doesn't work.
Write what you would key in to help you answer these questions.
You do not have to find the answers.

For example, to find 175×2, key in $175 + 175$;
to find 625×11, key in $6250 + 625$.

a 264×3

b 753×11

c $22 \times \square = 1034$

d 932×9

e $\square \times 72 = 2448$

f 36×101

g $367 \times 5 \times 2$

h 874×99

6 Say whether each statement below is true or false.
Give three examples for each.

a Dividing zero by a number always gives the answer zero.

b Multiplying a number by zero always gives the answer zero.

c Dividing a number by one always gives the number itself.

d Multiplying a number by one always gives the answer one.

e Dividing by a positive whole number greater than 1 always gives a smaller answer.

f Multiplying by a positive whole number always gives a smaller answer.

How did I do?

I know and can use the correct order of operations when calculating.

Teacher's tips

The 'O' in BODMAS stands for 'other', and includes squares, roots and powers (because BSRPDMAS is much harder to remember!). Don't forget to always do these before multiplication/division, and addition/subtraction.

You will revise:

▶ the correct order of operations in calculations.

Get started

As you saw in Unit 13, **BODMAS** will help you remember the order of operations in calculations. Use **BODMAS** to help you with the exercises in this unit.

Do anything in **brackets** first.
Next do **other** things such as squares, roots and powers.
Divide and **multiply** next.

Finally **add** and **subtract**.

Brackets
Other
Divide
Multiply
Add
Subtract

Practice

1 Work these out. Remember to use the order of BODMAS.

a $3 + 8 \times 6$
b $(7 + 9) \times 2$
c $36 \div 6 + 6$

d $24 - 14 \div 2$
e $28 \div 4 + 6$
f $27 \div (9 - 6)$

g $10 \times (7 - 2)$
h $(5 + 5)^2$
i $3 \times \sqrt{64}$

j $8 \times 2 + 5$
k $24 - 8 \div 2$
l $(19 - 9) \div 2$

m $(8 + 2) \times 5 + 5$
n $(2 + 8) \times (15 - 11)$
o $6 + 4^2$

Challenge

2 Work these out. One has been done for you.

a $\dfrac{9 + 15}{4 \times 2} = \dfrac{24}{8} = 3$
b $\dfrac{28 + 12}{3 + 7}$

c $\dfrac{130 - 10}{4 \times 2}$
d $\dfrac{3 \times 5}{10 \div 2}$

e $\dfrac{5^2 \times 4}{2 \times 5}$
f $\dfrac{15 - \sqrt{49}}{12 \div 3}$

g $\dfrac{3 \times 9}{27 - 18}$
h $\dfrac{56 \div 7}{36 \div 9}$

3 Work these out.

a $72 \div (3 + 6) - 7 + 3 \times (6 \div 3)^3$

b $(32 - 28) \div (3 - 1)^2 + 2^3 + 5 \times 8$

c $\dfrac{(2 \times -4)^2}{\sqrt{36} + 2^2}$

d $\dfrac{(-4)^2 \times 2}{4^3 \div \sqrt{64}}$

4 Make as many different answers as possible by putting brackets into each expression.

$4 \times 2 + 3 - 2^2 \times 7 + 1 =$ $4 \times 2 + 3 - 2^2 \times 7 + 1 =$

$4 \times 2 + 3 - 2^2 \times 7 + 1 =$ $4 \times 2 + 3 - 2^2 \times 7 + 1 =$

$4 \times 2 + 3 - 2^2 \times 7 + 1 =$ $4 \times 2 + 3 - 2^2 \times 7 + 1 =$

$4 \times 2 + 3 - 2^2 \times 7 + 1 =$ $4 \times 2 + 3 - 2^2 \times 7 + 1 =$

5 Work these out.

a $48 \div (7 + 5) - 8 + 2 \times (12 \div 6)^3$ **b** $18 \div (10 - 7)^2 + 5 \times \sqrt[3]{(4 \times 2)}$

c $6 + 2 \times (13 - 7)^2 - 5 \times \sqrt{100}$ **d** $(4 + 3)^2 - 4^3 \div 2 + (5 - 4)^3$

6 Use a calculator to work these out. Give your answers to two decimal places.

a $\dfrac{(7 + 1)^2 \, (3 + 2)^3}{(6 - 2)^2}$

b $\dfrac{(15 + 2)^2 \, (8 - 5)^2}{(8 + 2)^3}$

c $\dfrac{(13 - 6)^2 \, (5 + 2)^2}{(5 - 2)^3}$

d $\dfrac{(5 + 3)^2 \, (7 - 5)^3}{(6 - 3)^3}$

e $\dfrac{(15 - 9)^2 \, (8 - 5)^3}{\sqrt{28} + 32}$

f $\dfrac{(24 - 17)^2 \, (3 + 2)^2}{(7 - 2)^3}$

g $\dfrac{(16 - 9)^3 \times \sqrt{64}}{(17 - 9)^2}$

h $\dfrac{(12 - 9)^3 \, (1 + 2)^3}{\sqrt{27} + 56}$

i $\dfrac{(14 - 7)^2 \, (8 - 2)^2}{2(4 + 1)^3}$

j $\dfrac{(4 - 1)^2 \, (9 - 5)^2}{3(8 - 5)^3}$

How did I do?

I can use the correct order of operations when calculating.

Teacher's tips

Be methodical – follow BODMAS and rewrite the problem after solving each stage in turn so as to avoid making silly mistakes or getting lost. Better to take your time than be wrong!

15: Calculations and rounding

You will revise:
- rounding decimals to a number of decimal places
- approximating calculations by rounding each number to one significant figure.

Get started

When rounding a decimal to a number of decimal places (d.p.) your answer must always have that many digits after the decimal point. For example:

Round 42.5037 to 2 d.p. → 42.50

When rounding a number to one significant figure (1 s.f.) your answer must only have one digit that isn't zero. For example:

Round 42.5037 to one significant figure → 40

Round 0.004 74 to one significant figure → 0.005

When asked to estimate the size of the answer to a calculation, round the numbers to 1 significant figure before estimating. For example:

(4.06 × 7.985) ÷ 1.98 is approximately (4 × 8) ÷ 2 = 32 ÷ 2 = 16

Practice

1. Copy and complete this table.

Number	To the nearest whole number	To 1 d.p.	To 2 d.p.	To 3 d.p.
32.1502				
86.8309				
69.6065				
19.989				
6.4993				
0.0893				

Challenge

Try it yourself!

Which of these numbers is 40.58639 rounded to three significant figures?

40.5   40.586

40.59   40.6

40.587

2. Round these numbers to one significant figure.

a 746 867   b 2324   c 8594   d 57 858

e 5.376   f 23.48   g 5188.24   h 154.643

i 2846   j 876.8   k 4.756   l 16.656

m 3.81   n 18.6   o 26.48   p 705.12

3 Round these numbers less than 1 to one significant figure.

a 0.0067   b 0.0278   c 0.8594

d 0.000 058   e 0.057   f 0.45

g 0.796   h 0.0018   i 0.055 778

j 0.000 001 24   k 0.0457   l 0.0098

4 Round each number to one significant figure and find approximate answers to these.

a 6291×47

b $392 \div 8.1$

c $5.75 \times (9.46 - 6.48)$

d $8.34 \times (3.08 + 2.78)$

e $(7895 \div 1967) \times 2070$

f $\sqrt{(18.1 \times 1.98)} \times 19.89$

g $(0.011 \times 196)^2$

5 Round each number to one significant figure and find approximate answers to these.

a $(0.0075 \div 2.18) \times 6.8$

b $(0.5787 \div 2.69) \times 1.748$

c $0.0788 \times 0.0158 \times 0.391$

d $\dfrac{5.91 \times 4.09}{\sqrt{0.25}}$

e $\dfrac{0.041 \times 0.049}{(0.1)^2}$

f $(0.031 \times 19.6)^2$

g $\dfrac{(0.00381 \times 2031.6)^2}{0.814}$

How did I do?

I can round decimals to a given number of decimal places. ☐

I can approximate calculations by rounding each number to one significant figure. ☐

Teacher's tips

Rounding makes numbers easier to work with. Decimal places give a level of accuracy for fractions, whereas 'significant figure' is used for whole numbers. Remember with significant figures all digits become zero except the stated number of 'significant' digits.

16: Problem solving (1)

You will revise:
▶ how to solve word problems.

Get started

When faced with a problem to solve, follow these steps.

▶ Read the problem carefully.
▶ Look for any useful words in the question.
▶ Write down or circle any important numbers in the question.
▶ Decide what operations to use.
▶ Find an approximate answer.
▶ Decide whether to use a written or mental method and work it out.
▶ Finally check your answer.

Practice

1 Write whether you would use addition, subtraction, multiplication or division to answer these questions.

a James is 42 years old and his daughter is half his age. How old is she?

b Some children get into groups of 4. There are 8 groups. How many children are there?

c My dad has eight sweets. He shares them between four of us. How many do we each get?

d Fifteen people were on a bus. Eleven more got on. Now how many are on the bus?

e Jane has 24 stickers. Pete has 8 fewer. How many stickers has Pete?

Challenge

2 Solve these word problems.

a There are three times as many cars in a car park on Monday than on Sunday. 48 cars were parked there on Sunday. How many cars are there on Monday?

b 9543 people visited the Coliseum cinema this year. This was 2704 more than last year. How many people visited the cinema last year?

c Ella's mum is five times older than Ella. Ella's mum is 30. How old is Ella?

d There are 5 shelves. A supermarket has 20 tins of beans on each shelf. 32 tins get sold. How many tins are there now?

e   A car park has 785 spaces of which 57 are empty. How many cars are in the car park?

f   I had 49p. I was given 20p more. Then I spent 54p. How much do I have left?

g   25 cars are in the car park. 8 leave but 17 more arrive. How many cars are there now?

h   Amy saves £1.50 of her pocket money each week. After 10 weeks she buys a CD costing £10. How much money does she have left after that?

i   A teacher has 18 grey pencils and 15 coloured pencils. She gives away 6 pencils. How many pencils does she have in total now?

j   My mum is four times older than me. She is 36. How old will I be in 5 years?

k   My book has 48 pages. I have read 5 pages already. How many pages must I read to reach the middle of the book?

l   Six apples cost 66p. How much does it cost to buy 4 apples?

m   Jo buys a pencil costing 48p and a rubber costing 32p. How much less than £1 is this?

n   A burger costs £2.20. Mr Wildman buys four burgers for his children. How much change does he get from £10?

o   46 eggs are put into boxes that each hold 6 eggs. How many boxes are needed? How many boxes will be full?

p   A school has £62 to buy netballs. Each ball costs £4. How many can they buy?

q   45 children are going on a school trip. Each car can carry 4 children. How many cars will be needed?

r   One CD and a magazine costs £19. Four CDs and a magazine costs £58. What is the cost of one CD?

s   Which is greater: 25% of £5, or 75% of £1.60?

t   The value of a £140 000 house increased by 14% in May and by a further 9% in July. What was its new value?

u   In April, the cost of a new £125 tennis racket increased by 8%. Before the end of the season the new price was reduced by 15%. What was the end-of-season price?

You will revise:
▸ using the fraction keys on a calculator.

 Get started

To key a fraction or a mixed number into a calculator, use the $\boxed{a\frac{a}{b}}$ key.

To enter $\frac{7}{8}$:   Key in $\boxed{7}$ $\boxed{a\frac{a}{b}}$ $\boxed{8}$.   The display shows ⫪⌐8.

To enter $2\frac{3}{4}$:   Key in $\boxed{2}$ $\boxed{a\frac{a}{b}}$ $\boxed{3}$ $\boxed{a\frac{a}{b}}$ $\boxed{4}$.   The display shows 2⌐3⌐4.

If you press the $\boxed{=}$ key after entering the fraction, it will give it in its simplest form.

On some calculators, to convert a fraction to a decimal, key in the fraction and press the $\boxed{=}$ key. Then press the $\boxed{a\frac{b}{c}}$ key again. The display will show the decimal.

To convert a decimal to a fraction, key in the decimal and press the $\boxed{=}$ key. Then press the $\boxed{a\frac{b}{c}}$ key. The display will show the fraction.

Check that you know how to convert fractions to decimals (and vice versa) on your calculator.

 Practice

1 Use a calculator to find each fraction or mixed number in its simplest form.

a $\frac{120}{300}$ b $\frac{235}{500}$ c $\frac{480}{1080}$

d $\frac{450}{700}$ e $\frac{128}{512}$ f $\frac{64}{1024}$

g $5\frac{22}{32}$ h $8\frac{45}{50}$ i $9\frac{16}{36}$

j $5\frac{27}{63}$ k $3\frac{140}{490}$ l $2\frac{48}{64}$

 Challenge

2 Use a calculator to convert these fractions and mixed numbers to decimals.

a $\frac{7}{8}$ b $\frac{10}{8}$ c $\frac{1}{9}$

d $\frac{3}{9}$ e $\frac{7}{9}$ f $\frac{10}{9}$

g $\frac{15}{16}$ h $2\frac{3}{8}$ i $1\frac{2}{9}$

j $5\frac{4}{9}$ k $5\frac{7}{8}$ l $6\frac{8}{9}$

3 Without using a calculator predict what each of these fractions will be as a decimal. Use your answers to question 1 to help you.

a $\frac{2}{9}$

b $\frac{4}{9}$

c $1\frac{3}{4}$

d $\frac{6}{9}$

e $2\frac{5}{9}$

f $6\frac{1}{9}$

g $\frac{11}{9}$

h $\frac{3}{8}$

i $\frac{11}{8}$

4 Use a calculator to convert these decimals to fractions or mixed numbers, in their simplest form.

a 0.0625

b 9.075

c 3.284

d 0.1375

e 5.006

f 0.7225

g 8.125

h 0.8125

i 6.888

j 9.155

k 0.775

l 4.442

5 Use a calculator to help you explore and continue these patterns.

a $\frac{1}{11} = 0.0909090909\ldots$

$\frac{2}{11} = 0.1818181818\ldots$

$\frac{3}{11} = $ _____ $\ldots$

$\frac{4}{11} = $ _____ $\ldots$

$\frac{5}{11} = $ _____ $\ldots$

$\frac{6}{11} = $ _____ $\ldots$

$\frac{7}{11} = $ _____ $\ldots$

$\frac{8}{11} = $ _____ $\ldots$

$\frac{9}{11} = $ _____ $\ldots$

$\frac{10}{11} = $ _____ $\ldots$

b $\frac{1}{99} = 0.0101010101\ldots$

$\frac{2}{99} = 0.0202020202\ldots$

$\frac{3}{99} = $ _____ $\ldots$

$\frac{4}{99} = $ _____ $\ldots$

$\frac{5}{99} = $ _____ $\ldots$

$\frac{6}{99} = $ _____ $\ldots$

$\frac{7}{99} = $ _____ $\ldots$

$\frac{8}{99} = $ _____ $\ldots$

$\frac{9}{99} = $ _____ $\ldots$

$\frac{10}{99} = $ _____ $\ldots$

6 Without using a calculator predict the answers to these. Give your answers as fractions or mixed numbers.

a $\frac{1}{11} + \frac{1}{99}$

b $\frac{2}{11} + \frac{2}{99}$

c $\frac{1}{11} - \frac{1}{99}$

d $\frac{1}{11} \div \frac{2}{99}$

e $\frac{9}{11} \div \frac{2}{99}$

f $\frac{1}{11} - \frac{4}{99}$

Now use a calculator to check your answers.

How did I do?

I can use a calculator to answer questions involving fractions and decimals.

Teacher's tips

Always press the C/AC button first when using a calculator to clear previous work.
Enter the information methodically; just one small mistake will give the wrong answer.
Always estimate the answer in your head to check that the calculator's answer looks right.

You will revise:
▶ how to solve word problems.

Get started

When faced with a problem to solve, follow these steps.

▶ Read the problem carefully.
▶ Look for any useful words in the question.
▶ Write down or circle any important numbers in the question.
▶ Decide what operations to use.
▶ Find an approximate answer.
▶ Decide whether to use a written or a mental method and work it out.
▶ Finally check your answer.

Practice

1 Solve these problems.

a I had 69p. I was given 20p more and then I spent 78p. How much do I have left?

b 125 cars were in the car park. 18 left but 34 more arrived. How many cars are there now?

c Amy saves £3.50 of her pocket money each week. After 10 weeks she decides to buy a CD costing £13. How much money does she have left after that?

d My mum is three times older than me. She is 42. How old was she when I was born?

e My book has 96 pages. I have read 17 pages already. How many pages must I read to reach the middle of the book?

f Six apples cost 84p. How much do five apples cost?

Challenge

2 Solve these problems.

a A school has 134 Year 7 pupils and 150 Year 8 pupils. There are half as many Year 9 pupils as there are in Years 7 and 8 put together. How many pupils are there in Years 7, 8 and 9 altogether?

b In a different school the ratio of Year 7 pupils to Year 8 pupils is 3 : 4. If there are 210 Year 7 pupils, how many pupils are in Year 8?

c 345 children are going on a school trip. Each coach can carry 49 children. How many coaches will be needed?

d A chocolate factory makes 583 chocolates. 20 chocolates are put into each box. How many full boxes of chocolates can be made?

e Mr Wood runs at 16 kilometres per hour. During one month he ran a total of 220 kilometres. For approximately how many hours did he run?

3 Solve these problems.

a In another three years Jack will be three times as old as he was three years ago. How old is Jack now?

b A market stall holder bought 120 green apples at '4 for a pound' and 120 red apples at '6 for a pound'. Would it have been cheaper, more expensive or the same, if she had bought 240 apples at '10 for a pound'?

c Which is less: 40% of £160 or 75% of £80?

d Which is greater: 25% of £2.60 or 90% of £0.60?

e The value of a £260 000 house increased by 14% in May and by a further 7% in July. What was its new value?

4 Solve these puzzles.

a The difference between the ages of two people is 44. The same two ages are multiplied to give the answer 1280. What are the ages of the people?

b Partition the number 46 into two parts, so that if one part is divided by 7 and the other part is divided by 3, the sum of the results will be 10.

c In a room there are some fish and some people. There are 20 eyes and 14 legs. How many fish are there?

d In a field there are some cows and some people. There are 36 legs and 12 heads. How many cows are there?

e In a room there are some cats and some people. There are 16 eyes and 8 hands. How many cats are there?

f In a room there are some fish, some dogs and some people. There are 28 legs, 24 eyes, 12 mouths and 8 tails. How many
  i fish, ii dogs, iii people are there?

> **Try it yourself!**
>
> I am thinking of a number less than 100. If I divide the number by 2, by 3, by 4, by 5 or by 6, I always have 1 left over. What is my number?

> **How did I do?**
>
> I can solve word problems. ☐

Teacher's tips

In more complex word problems you still need to translate to a number sentence (using the tips as before), but you may also need to include brackets around some parts to show they happen independently. Remember to then use BODMAS.

19: Trial and improvement

You will revise:
- using trial and improvement methods.

 **Get started**

Trial and improvement methods involve making an estimate and using it to get closer to the actual answer. By repeating this process many times you can get very close to the answer or actually reach it.

This table shows how an estimate of the value of x (to two decimal places) can be found for $x^3 = 50$.

$x^3 = 50$

x	x^3	Too large/small?	Comments
3.5	42.875	Too small	Choose a number larger than 3.5 such as 3.7.
3.7	50.653	Too large	Choose a number smaller than 3.7 but larger than 3.5.
3.6	46.656	Too small	Choose a number larger than 3.6 but smaller than 3.7.
3.65	48.627 125	Too small	Choose a number larger than 3.65 but smaller than 3.7.
3.68	49.836 032	Too small	Choose a number larger than 3.68 but smaller than 3.7.
3.69	50.243 409	Too large	Choose a number smaller than 3.69 but larger than 3.68.
3.685	50.039 44 . . .	Too large	This tells you that it is closer to 3.68 than 3.69.

So $x = 3.68$ (to 2 d.p.)

 **Practice**

1 Do not use a calculator. Which two whole numbers must each unknown lie between? Write each answer like this: a must lie between _____ and _____.

a $a = \sqrt{80}$　　　　　　　**b** $b = \sqrt{32}$

c $c^2 = 93$　　　　　　　　**d** $x^2 = 14$

Challenge

2 Estimate the value of x to two decimal places for which $x^2 = 14$. Draw a table like this, but with as many rows as you need. You may use the square key on the calculator but not the square-root key.

$x^2 = 14$

x	x^2	Too large/small?

3 Do not use a calculator. Which two whole numbers must each cube root lie between? Write each answer like this: *a* must lie between _____ and _____.

a $a = \sqrt[3]{34}$

b $b = \sqrt[3]{23}$

c $c^3 = 6$

d $x^3 = 54$

4 Estimate the value of *x* to two decimal places for which $x^3 = 54$. Draw a table like this, but with as many rows as you need. You may use the cube key on the calculator but not the cube-root key.

$$x^3 = 54$$

x	x^2	Too large/small?

5 Estimate the value of *x* to two decimal places for which $x^3 - x = 102$. Draw a table like this, but with as many rows as you need.

$$x^3 - x = 102$$

x	x^3	$x^3 - x$	Too large/small?

Try it yourself!

A number when doubled and then squared gives the same result as the number cubed. If the number is not zero, what is the number?

6 Estimate the value of *x* to two decimal places for which $x^3 + x^2 = 289$. Draw your own table. Begin with a number between 6 and 7.

How did I do?

I can use trial and improvement methods to find solutions to equations to a given degree of accuracy.

Teacher's tips

Systematically narrow down a range of possible answers. Start with values that you do know, that are as close to the answer as possible. Make basic estimates mentally, then more accurate ones with a calculator.

20: Simplifying expressions (1)

You will revise:
▶ how to simplify algebraic expressions
▶ how to expand brackets by multiplying out expressions.

 Get started

Simplifying means writing something more simply. When an expression is simplified, it is written as simply as possible, where like terms have been collected together and repeated multiplications written using powers.

Expanding an expression means writing it without brackets as simply as possible.

 **Practice**

1 Simplify these expressions by collecting like terms.
For example, $p + 3p + 4q - q = 4p + 3q$

a $5y - 2y + 2x - x + 3y$

b $6m + 5n - 5m - 2n$

c $9s + t + t - t - 4s$

d $6e + 6f + e - 4f - e$

e $8j + 3k - 3j + k - 2k$

f $7c + 2d - c - 2d - 3d$

g $6v + w + 2w - 5v - 2w$

 Challenge

2 Simplify these expressions by collecting like terms.

a $m + 3m + n + 4 - 2n + 3 + m - 4n$

b $2s + 5t + t + 5 + 2 - s + s - 3t$

c $g + 4g + 7 + h + 1 - 2h - 2$

d $5x + 3 - 2x - 6 + 3y + y$

e $4 + 2c + 3d - c - 2 - 3d - 5$

f $8s - 3t + 2 + 4t - 5 - 2s$

g $e + e - e + f - 2f + 7f + 2 + 6 - 5$

h $2j - 5k + k + 3 - 8j + 5k - 2j - 4 + 1$

3 Find the perimeter of each shape. Simplify the answer as much as possible.

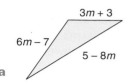
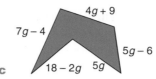

a **b** **c**

4 Expand these brackets.

a $5(3a - 2)$ **b** $6(2m + 3)$ **c** $7(p + 5)$

d $8(3y - 4)$ **e** $10(2 - n)$ **f** $4(7 - 6f)$

5 Expand the brackets and simplify the result.

a $3(a + 4) + 2(2a - 1)$ **b** $4(m + 3) + 7(3 - m)$

c $3(p + 5) + 4(5p - 1)$ **d** $8(2y + 1) + 3(2 - 3y)$

6 Simplify each expression. Notice that some expressions are additions and some are multiplications.

a $b \times b \times b \times b$

b $a \times a \times a \times a \times a$

c $g + g + g$

d $m + m + m + m$

e $n \times n \times n \times n \times n \times n$

f $s + s + s + s + s$

g $t + t + t$

h $w \times w \times w \times w$

i $e \times e \times e \times e \times e \times e \times e$

j $y \times y \times y \times y \times y \times y$

k $v + v + v + v + v + v + v + v$

l $p \times p \times p$

m $f + f + f + f + f + f + f$

n $j \times j \times j \times j \times j \times j \times j \times j \times j$

o $k \times k \times k \times k \times k$

> **Try it yourself!**
>
> Write four expressions that could be simplified to the expression:
> $8x - 2y - 4$.

7 Expand the brackets and simplify. Remember that, once expanded, both parts of the second bracket must be subtracted from the first bracket.

a $7(a + 4) - 2(2a + 1)$ **b** $3(m + 3) - 4(3m + 2)$

c $5(p + 5) - 4(5p + 1)$ **d** $6(2y + 1) - 3(2 + 3y)$

e $8(3q + 1) - 4(1 + 4q)$

> **How did I do?**
>
> I can simplify algebraic expressions. ☐
>
> I can expand brackets by multiplying out expressions. ☐

Teacher's tips

Be very careful to write and solve algebraic problems accurately. A common error is to think that $a + a + a = a^3$; this is wrong, $a + a + a = 3a$ ($a^3 = a \times a \times a$).

21: Simplifying expressions (2)

You will revise:
- simplifying, expanding and factorising algebraic expressions.

 Get started

Simplifying means writing something more simply. When an expression is simplified, it is written as simply as possible, where like terms have been collected together and repeated multiplications written using powers.

Expanding an expression means writing it without brackets as simply as possible.

The opposite of expanding brackets is called **factorising**. Factorising means finding factors that divide into each part of the expression.

For example, $15ay + 6by$ when factorised is $3y(5a + 2b)$ as $3y$ is a factor of both $15ay$ and $6by$.

 Practice

1 Expand these brackets.

   a $4(3a - 2)$ **b** $9(2m + 3)$

   c $2(p + 5)$ **d** $5(3y - 4)$

   e $8(2 - n)$ **f** $6(7 - 6f)$

   g $10(7 - 2m)$ **h** $2(12 - 3b)$

Challenge

2 Expand and simplify these.

   a $9(p + 4) + 3(4p + 1)$ **b** $6(e - 1) + 3(e + 5)$

   c $8(m - 1) + 7(6 + m)$ **d** $7(2n + 3) + 2(4 + 3n)$

   e $10(a - 4) + 3(2a + 6)$ **f** $5(3y - 1) + 3(2y - 1)$

   g $5(3y + 3) + 2(4y - 5)$ **h** $9(2g + 4) + 3(2 - 3g)$

3 Expand and simplify these.

   a $10(p + 4) - 3(4p + 1)$ **b** $7(3e - 1) - 3(5e + 2)$

   c $6(m - 1) - 2(6 - m)$ **d** $5(n + 3) - 2(3 - 2n)$

4 Expand these brackets.

    a $4b(2a - 4c)$ **b** $6k(2p + 3)$

    c $2p(p + 5q)$ **d** $10y(3y - 1)$

    e $8n(2 - n)$ **f** $-3xy(x + 3y)$

    g $-2e(7f - 3e)$ **h** $-5x(5x - 1)$

5 Factorise these expressions by taking a factor outside a pair of brackets. For example, $5a + 15 = 5(a + 3)$.

    a $4p + 8$ **b** $6d + 3e$

    c $9m + 6n$ **d** $2x + 12y$

    e $30p + 10q$ **f** $18a - 21b$

    g $16p - 20r$ **h** $10s - 8t$

6 Factorise these expressions by taking a factor outside a pair of brackets.

    a $n^2 - n$ **b** $3a + 5ab$

    c $5de + 15e$ **d** $9c + 6c^2$

    e $2xy + 8y$ **f** $10abc + 10cd$

    g $4m - 12m^2$ **h** $5x^2 - 15x$

    i $10st + 5t$ **j** $15pq - 5p$

    k $6t - 6$ **l** $8g - 18g^2$

> **Try it yourself!**
>
> Write four expressions that could be factorised fully to the expression $8x(x - 2y)$.

> **How did I do?**
>
>   ✔
>
> I can simplify algebraic expressions. ☐
>
> I can expand expressions by multiplying out brackets. ☐
>
> I can factorise expressions. ☐

Teacher's tips

The most common mistake when factorising and expanding is to not do the same thing to every value in the brackets, for instance $3(5a + 2) = 15a + 6$ (not $15a + 2$), because everything inside the bracket has to be multiplied by the 3.

22: Problem solving (3)

You will revise:
▶ how to solve word problems.

 Get started

When faced with a problem to solve, follow these steps.

▶ Read the problem carefully.
▶ Look for any useful words in the question.
▶ Write down or circle any important numbers in the question.
▶ Decide what operations to use.
▶ Find an approximate answer.
▶ Decide whether to use a written or a mental method and work it out.
▶ Finally check your answer.

Practice

1 Solve these word problems.

a In another 4 years Jack will be three times as old as he was 8 years ago. How old is Jack now?

b A market stall holder bought 100 green apples at '4 for a pound' and 120 red apples at '6 for a pound'. Would it have been cheaper, more expensive or the same, if she had bought 220 apples at '5 for a pound'?

c Which is less: 70% of 50 km or 75% of 45 km?

d Which is more: 36% of 40 kg or 41% of 35 kg?

e The value of a £260 000 house increased by 6% in May and by a further 8% in July. What was its new value?

Challenge

Try it yourself!

I think of a number. All except two of 1 to 10 are factors of this number. The two numbers that are not factors are consecutive. What is the smallest number I could be thinking of?

2 Solve these puzzles.

a The difference between the ages of two people is 9. The same two ages are multiplied to give the answer 442. Are both people over the age of 18?

b Partition the number 52 into two parts, so that each part is a square number.

c Partition the number 205 into two parts, so that each part is a square number.

d Find the smallest number greater than 45 that has the same number of factors as 45.

3 Solve these puzzles.

a What fraction is halfway between $\frac{4}{5}$ and $\frac{7}{8}$?

b A number is a multiple of 24 and 32, and has four digits. What is the smallest number it could be?

c Two families went to the cinema. The Jones family bought tickets for one adult and four children and paid £20. The Mills family bought tickets for two adults and two children and paid £19. What was the cost of one child's ticket?

d The diagram shows two identical overlapping rectangles. 25% of each rectangle is shaded. What fraction of the whole diagram is shaded?

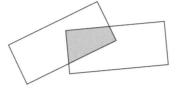

e In a room there are some fish, some dogs and some people. There are 30 legs, 32 eyes, 16 mouths and 13 tails. How many
i fish, **ii** dogs, **iii** people are there?

f A plank of wood weighed 2.8 kg. 25 centimetres of the plank were cut off its length. The plank then weighed 1.6 kg. What was the length of the original plank?

4 Solve these puzzles.

a Take a two-digit number. Reverse the digits. Is it possible to make a number that is one-and-a-half times as big as the original number?

b Take a two-digit number. Reverse the digits. Is it possible to make a number that is one-and-three-quarters times as big as the original number?

c A tractor has two large wheels and two small wheels. The large wheels have a diameter of 180 cm and the diameter of the small wheels is 50 cm. When the tractor is stationary, the wheels are marked at a point where each touches the ground. The tractor is driven off in a straight line. After what distance do all the marks first touch the ground at the same moment?

d The diagram shows two identical small circles inside a large circle. Is it true that the circumference of each smaller circle is exactly half the circumference of the larger circle?

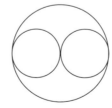

How did I do?

I can solve word problems. ✔ ☐

Teacher's tips

When a word problem expresses a relationship between unknown numbers use algebra to translate it into a number sentence and then solve it. So question 1a can be expressed as:
$a + 4 = 3(a - 8)$

You will revise:

▶ how to solve equations with one unknown.

Get started

An **equation** always has an equals sign, as in $2y + 3 = 4y - 1$. What is on one side of the equals sign is worth the same as what is on the other side.

When there is only one unknown in an equation, it is possible to **solve** the equation. This means finding out what number the letter stands for.

Practice

1 Use a calculator to help you solve these equations. Some have decimal answers.

a $2a + 9 = 27$

b $8y - 6 = 41$

c $5f - 16 = 31$

d $4y + 12 = 29$

e $57 = 8n + 4$

f $17 = 5g - 4$

Challenge

2 Use a calculator to help you solve these equations. Some have decimal answers. Round answers if necessary.

a $7(h - 1) = 28$

b $6(k + 3) = 72$

c $8(c - 4) = 64$

d $31 = 5(g + 7)$

e $39 = 4(17 - x)$

f $23 = 2(42 - p)$

g $2(h - 3) = 21$

h $4(j + 8) = 53$

i $5(2k - 1) = 26$

j $3(m - 2) = 19$

k $25 = 12f + 1$

l $6(3p - 7) = 73$

3 Solve these equations. You may use a calculator. Some have decimal answers.

a $7f - 12 = 3f - 4$

b $7b - 4 = 5b + 6$

c $7d - 3 = 3d + 7$

d $8a - 3 = 6a + 7$

e $11e - 6 = 5e + 9$

f $8c - 4 = 7c + 1$

g $6g + 1 = 5g + 8$

h $7h - 5 = 5h + 2$

i $6j - 1 = 3j + 6$

j $2m - 1 = 8m + 7$

k $25 - p = 9p + 4$

l $7s - 4 = 29 - 4s$

4 Solve these equations. You may use a calculator. Some have decimal answers.

a $4(r - 8) = 16 - r$

b $5(t + 2) = 2t + 6$

c $8u - 6 = 9(u - 2)$

d $9 - 3m = 6(m + 4)$

e $8(5 + k) = 7k - 5$

f $21 - 2n = 7(n - 10)$

5 The lengths of rectangles are shown as expressions. Write an equation for each rectangle and solve it. Use your answer to find the length of each rectangle.

$5(2m + 7)$

a

$2(6m + 1)$

$9(3s - 5)$

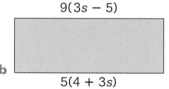

b

$5(4 + 3s)$

$2(5 - 2n)$

c

$6(4 + 2n)$

How did I do?

I can solve equations with one unknown.

Teacher's tips

Use BODMAS. Once the equation is expanded and simplified the substitute can be made the subject (isolated like a =) by doing inverse operations to remove the other elements of the equation. Remember to do the same to both sides.

24: Formulae and substituting (1)

You will revise:
- deriving and using formulae
- substituting values into a formula.

Get started

To **substitute** means to exchange (or replace) one thing for another. In sport, players are substituted. In maths, numbers are substituted for letters.

A **formula** is a way of writing a mathematical rule, showing the relationship between things. For example, this formula shows the relationship between the area of a rectangle and its length and width:

Area of a rectangle = length $\times$ width $A = l \times w$

Values can be substituted into the formula to find an unknown.

Practice

1 A bookshop sells books costing £2 each. A formula for the cost (C) can be written as $C = 2n$, where n is the number of books bought.

Use the formula to find the cost C when:

a 3 books were bought, $n = 3$ **b** 4 books were bought, $n = 4$

c 8 books were bought, $n = 8$ **d** 11 books were bought, $n = 11$

e 9 books were bought, $n = 9$ **f** 15 books were bought, $n = 15$

Challenge

2 A theme park has an entrance fee of £5. Each ride at the fair costs £3. A formula for the cost (C) can be written as $C = 5 + 3n$, where n is the number of rides.

Use the formula to find the cost C when:

a $n = 3$ **b** $n = 4$ **c** $n = 7$ **d** $n = 6$

e $n = 5$ **f** $n = 10$ **g** $n = 8$ **h** $n = 12$

3 Substitute these values of y into $P = 6y + 1$ to find the value of P.

a $y = 3$ **b** $y = 4$ **c** $y = 10$

4 Substitute these values of m and n into $R = 10m - 2n$ to find the value of R.

a $m = 3$ and $n = 1$ b $m = 5$ and $n = 8$

c $m = 6$ and $n = 3$ d $m = 1$ and $n = 5$

5 The formula $P \approx L \div 4 \times 7$ can be used to convert (approximately) between litres and pints, where L is the number of litres and P is the number of pints.

Convert these amounts to pints using the formula $P \approx L \div 4 \times 7$.

a $L = 8$ litres   b $L = 12$ litres   c $L = 24$ litres

d $L = 28$ litres   e $L = 32$ litres   f $L = 44$ litres

g $L = 80$ litres   h $L = 100$ litres   i $L = 48$ litres

6 Use the formula $T = D \div S$ to calculate the time T (in seconds) it takes to travel a distance D (in metres) at a particular speed S (in m/s). You may use a calculator.

a $D = 722$ m, $S = 38$ m/s   b $D = 756$ m, $S = 42$ m/s

c $D = 840$ m, $S = 35$ m/s   d $D = 1014$ m, $S = 39$ m/s

e $D = 1645$ m, $S = 47$ m/s

7 Which of the following formulae gives the highest value of W when:

a $n = 2$ b $n = 3$ c $n = 4$ d $n = 5$

A $W = 2n + 1$ **B** $W = 12 - 2n$ **C** $W = 5n - 3$

D $W = \frac{1}{2}(n + 2)$ **E** $W = n^2$ **F** $W = 3(7 - n)$ **G** $W = 2(n + 4)$

8 This fence is made from identical planks of wood. Each fence post is one metre from the next.

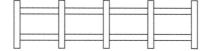

Write a formula for the number of planks P needed to make a fence that is N metres long.

Use this pattern to help you:

$N = 1$, $P = 4$

$N = 2$, $P = 7$

$N = 3$, $P = 10$

How did I do?

I can derive and use formulae from mathematics and other subjects. ☐

I can substitute values into a formula. ☐

Teacher's tips

The letter chosen as the substitute is not important as it represents an unknown value rather than a unit. However, answers should still be shown with the correct unit notation when appropriate.

You will revise:
- substituting values into formulae
- changing the subject of a formula.

Get started

To **substitute** means to exchange (or replace) one thing for another. In sport, players are substituted. In maths, numbers are substituted for letters.

A **formula** is a way of writing a mathematical rule that shows the relationship between things.

Changing the subject of the formula means rewriting it in a way so that the formula is expressed in terms of a different variable. For example, to change the subject of the formula $F = ma$ to m means rewriting it as $m = \dfrac{F}{a}$. For example:

$P = 2(l + w)$
P = perimeter of a rectangle, l = length, w = width
Change the subject to w.

$P = 2l + 2w$
$P - 2l = 2w$
$\dfrac{P - 2l}{2} = w$ so $w = \dfrac{P - 2l}{2}$

Practice

1 Substitute to find the value of each expression when $x = 3$. You may use a calculator.

   a $7(3 + x^2)$ **b** $11 - 2x^2$ **c** $(2x - 3)^3$

   d $(2x - 4)^2 + 36$ **e** $3x^2 - (8 - x)$ **f** $5x^3 + 6x$

   g $10 + 4x^2$ **h** $2(x + 2)^2 - 10x$ **i** $1 + \dfrac{x^3}{2}$

Challenge

2 Use the formula in each part to answer each question, rounding your answers to 2 d.p.

   a $A = \pi r^2$
      A = area of a circle, π = pi ≈ 3.14 and r = radius
      Find the area A of a circle with a radius of 7.5 cm.

   b $V = l^3$
      V = volume of a cube, l = length of a side
      Find the volume V of a cube with sides of length 4.5 cm.

c $c = \sqrt{(a^2 + b^2)}$

c = hypotenuse of a right-angled triangle, and a and b are the shorter two sides.

Find the hypotenuse c of a right-angled triangle with shorter sides a and b of lengths 5 cm and 12 cm.

d $S = 2bl + 2lh + 2hb$

S = surface area of a cuboid, l = length, b = breadth, h = height.

Find the surface area, S, of a cuboid of length 3.2 cm, breadth 2 cm and height 6 cm.

3 Here are some formulae used in mathematics and in science. Rewrite each formula to change the subject to the letter shown.

a $S = D/T$

S = average speed, D = distance, T = time.

Change the subject to D.

b $F = ma$

F = force, m = mass, a = acceleration.

Change the subject to a.

c $A = \pi r^2$

A = area of a circle, π = pi $\approx$ 3.14, r = radius.

Change the subject to r.

d $v = u + at$

u = initial speed, v = speed after t seconds, t = time, a = acceleration.

Change the subject to a.

e $V = l^3$

V = volume of a cube, l = length of a side.

Change the subject to l.

4 Make C the subject of the formula $F = \dfrac{9C}{5} + 32$.

5 Make r the subject of the formula $V = \dfrac{4\pi r^3}{3}$.

6 Make l the subject of the formula $T = 2\pi \sqrt{\dfrac{l}{g}}$.

Try it yourself!

Make u the subject of the formula:

$\dfrac{1}{v} + \dfrac{1}{u} = \dfrac{1}{f}$.

How did I do?

✔

I can substitute values into formulae. ☐

I can change the subject of a formula. ☐

Teacher's tips

To change the subject of an equation, first expand then simplify the equation, then do inverse operations to eliminate the other elements of the equation on the same side as the target subject. Remember, square root is the inverse of squared.

You will revise:

▶ generating sequences from given rules and *n*th terms

▶ describing sequences using rules and *n*th terms.

Get started

Numbers arranged in a special order are called **sequences**. Each number in a sequence is called a **term**. There are two ways of describing sequences.

The **term-to-term rule** describes the first term and how each term is different from the previous term.

3, 7, 11, 15, 19, 23, . . .
The first term is 3. Each term increases by 4.

The **position-to-term rule** describes how to work out each term from where it is in the sequence, its position. For example, for this sequence, the position-to-term rule is: multiply the position number by 4 and subtract 1.

Position number (*n*)	1	2	3	4	5	6
Term	3	7	11	15	19	23

The position-to-term rule is sometimes given as a formula for the **nth term**. For this sequence, the *n*th term is $4n - 1$.

Practice

1 Write the first five terms of these sequences.

  a Multiply the position number by 5 and add 4; *n*th term = $5n + 4$.

  b Multiply the position number by 3 and subtract 3; *n*th term = $3n - 3$.

  c Multiply the position number by 2 and subtract the answer from 16; *n*th term = $16 - 2n$.

Challenge

2 Generate the first five terms of each of these sequences.

  a *n*th term = $5n$ **b** *n*th term = $5n + 2$ **c** *n*th term = $5n - 1$

3 Write the rule for the *n*th term for each sequence. State the 10th term of the sequence.

a

Position number (*n*)	1	2	3	4	5	6
Term	6	12	18	24	30	36

b

Position number (n)	1	2	3	4	5	6
Term	2	4	6	8	10	12

c

Position number (n)	1	2	3	4	5	6
Term	8	16	24	32	40	48

d

Position number (n)	1	2	3	4	5	6
Term	6	11	16	21	26	31

4 **a** Count how many **grey** squares each shape has to create a sequence. Do not count the white squares.

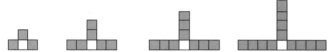

   b Write the rule for the *n*th term of the sequence.

   c Write the number of grey squares used to make the 10th shape in the sequence.

5 **a** Count how many **grey and white** squares each shape has to create a sequence.

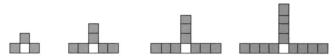

   b Write the rule for the *n*th term of the sequence.

   c Write the number of squares altogether used to make the 10th shape in the sequence.

6 Write the position-to-term rule to show the number of grey and white squares in the *n*th pattern of this sequence.

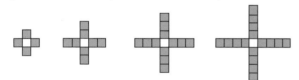

7 Write a sequence to match each of these descriptions. Then state the term-to-term rule and the position-to-term rule.

   a Each term is a multiple of 3.

   b Each term is an odd number.

   c Each term ends with the digit 7.

How did I do?

✔

I can generate and describe sequences. ☐

I can find and use *n*th terms of sequences. ☐

Teacher's tips

The first term in a sequence can be any number, so a sequence often has a term-to-term increase of '*a*' but does not follow the '*a*' times table. Generate a formula for the sequence to make it easier to calculate any term.

You will revise:

▶ how to find the *n*th term of a sequence.

Get started

Numbers arranged in a special order are called **sequences**. Each number in a sequence is called a **term**. There are two ways of describing sequences.

The **term-to-term rule** describes the first term and how each term is different from the previous term.

The **position-to-term rule** describes how to work out each term from where it is in the sequence, its position. The position-to-term rule is sometimes given as a formula for the **nth term**.

How to find the *n*th term:

1. Find the difference between adjacent (next-door) numbers in the sequence. If the difference is the same this tells you which times table the sequence is related to.
2. Write out the related times table under the sequence.
3. Then compare each number in the times table with the related number in the sequence.
4. Write the rule in symbols, with the times-table number showing the number of *n* (such as 2*n* for the 2 times table).

Here is an example.

Find the rule for the *n*th term of this sequence: 7, 9, 11, 13, 15, 17, . . .

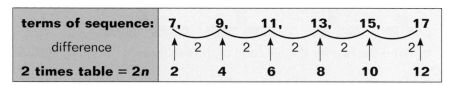

terms of sequence:	7,	9,	11,	13,	15,	17
difference		2	2	2	2	2
2 times table = 2*n*	2	4	6	8	10	12

Notice that each number in the sequence is 5 more than 2*n*, so the *n*th term is 2*n* + 5.

Practice

1 Generate the first five terms of each of these sequences.

    a *n*th term = 7*n*

    b *n*th term = 7*n* + 2

    c *n*th term = 7*n* − 1

Challenge

2 Find the rule for the *n*th term for each sequence.

a

Terms of sequence	4	10	16	22	28	34	. . .

b

Terms of sequence	2	7	12	17	22	27	. . .

c

Terms of sequence	12	14	16	18	20	24	. . .

d

Terms of sequence	3	10	17	24	31	38	. . .

e

Terms of sequence	−9	−5	−1	3	7	10	. . .

f

Terms of sequence	1	3	5	7	9	11	. . .

3 Now write the 100th term of each of the sequences in question 2.

4 Find the rule for the *n*th term. Each sequence is related to the sequence n^2 (the sequence of square numbers 1, 4, 9, 16, 25, . . .).

a

Terms of sequence	2	5	10	17	26	37	. . .

b

Terms of sequence	2	8	18	32	50	72	. . .

c

Terms of sequence	−1	2	7	14	23	34	. . .

d

Terms of sequence	5	20	45	80	125	180	. . .

5 Now write the 10th term of each of the sequences in question 4.

Try it yourself!

The 1st term of a sequence is 6 and the 10th term is 42. What could be the rule for the *n*th term of the sequence?

How did I do?

I can find the *n*th term of a sequence by looking at the pattern of differences between adjacent terms.

Teacher's tips

Use the sequence and position number table to generate a formula for '*n*', which is: (the term-to-term change x *n*) + (the difference between '*n*' and the first term). Check your formula against the sequence.

You will revise:
- mapping diagrams
- combining functions
- inverse functions.

Get started

A **function** turns one number into another. Functions can be described in words, for example 'multiply by 3 and then add 2', or using symbols: $x \rightarrow 3x + 2$.

The table below shows some outcomes for the function $x \rightarrow 3x + 2$.

INPUT x	1	2	3	4	5	6
OUTPUT $3x + 2$	5	8	11	14	17	20

Functions can also be shown on mapping diagrams, as below. Two lines make up a mapping diagram, one for the input number and the other for the output number. Arrows are used to join each input with its related output number.

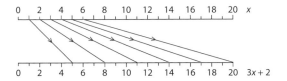

Practice

1 Copy and complete each input/output table.
Then draw a mapping diagram for each table using scales from 0 to 10.

a $x \rightarrow 3x - 3$

INPUT x	1	2	3	4	5	6
OUTPUT $3x - 3$						

b $x \rightarrow 2(x - 1)$

INPUT x	1	2	3	4	5	6
OUTPUT $2(x - 1)$						

Challenge

2 **a** Copy and complete this two-tiered mapping diagram for the
function $x \rightarrow 2x - 1$ followed by the function $x \rightarrow \dfrac{(x + 1)}{2}$.

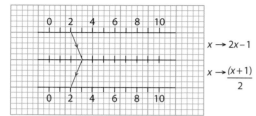

$x \rightarrow 2x - 1$

$x \rightarrow \dfrac{(x + 1)}{2}$

b Are these functions inverses of each other?

3 **a** Draw a two-tiered mapping diagram for the function $x \rightarrow 9 - x$
followed by the function $x \rightarrow 9 - x$.

b Are these functions inverses of each other?

c A function that has an inverse that is the same as itself is called
a 'self-inverse' function. Is the function $x \rightarrow 10 - x$ a self-inverse
function?

4 Give the inverse of each of these functions.

a $x \rightarrow 2x + 1$ **b** $x \rightarrow 3x - 2$

c $x \rightarrow \frac{1}{2}x - 5$ **d** $x \rightarrow 6(4 + x)$

e $x \rightarrow 8x + 4$ **f** $x \rightarrow 7x - 3$

g $x \rightarrow \frac{1}{4}x + 1$ **h** $x \rightarrow 3(x + 1)$

i $x \rightarrow 5 - 2x$ **j** $x \rightarrow \frac{1}{4}x + 5$

k $x \rightarrow \dfrac{x + 4}{3}$ **l** $x \rightarrow \dfrac{2x - 6}{10}$

> **Try it yourself!**
>
> What is special about these
> self-inverse functions?

5 Check your answers to question 4 by drawing two-tiered mapping
diagrams or by choosing different values of x to input.

> **How did I do?**
>
>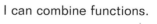
>
> I can represent functions as mapping diagrams.
>
> I can combine functions.
>
> I can find the inverse of a function.

Teacher's tips

A function relates an input into an output – think of it as the instruction to a machine that
always does the same thing. The more input the more output, but always in the same ratio
following the same function.

You will revise:

▸ functions that produce straight-line graphs

▸ how to plot the graphs of linear functions in the form $y = mx + c$.

Get started

Functions can be drawn as graphs on a coordinate grid.

Linear functions are those that produce straight lines.

All horizontal lines on a grid are 'y = a number'. To find what the number is, see where the line crosses the y-axis.

All vertical lines on a grid are 'x = a number'. To find what the number is, see where the line crosses the x-axis.

All diagonal lines on a grid have functions that include x and y. The functions can be arranged into the form $y = mx + c$, where m and c are numbers.

▸ The **gradient** of the straight line (how steep it is) is the value of m.

▸ The point where the line crosses the y-axis (the y **intercept**) is the value of c.

Practice

1 State whether each function produces a vertical, horizontal or diagonal line when plotted as a straight-line graph. For example, $y = 5$ produces a horizontal line.

a $y = 2x + 1$ **b** $y = 5x$

c $x = -3$ **d** $x = 2$

e $2x - 3 = y$ **f** $y = 5x - 1$

g $y = -2$ **h** $x = y$

i $x = 0$ **j** $y = -x$

Challenge

Try it yourself!

The line $x = y$ goes diagonally at 45° to the horizontal, from bottom left to top right of a square coordinate grid, through the origin. What is the equation of the line that is the reflection of this line in the y-axis?

2 **a** Copy and complete this table for $y = 2x + 3$.
Write the set of coordinates produced.

x	−2	−1	0	1	2
$y = 2x + 3$	−1				

b Copy the graph axes on to grid paper, plot the coordinates and label the line correctly.

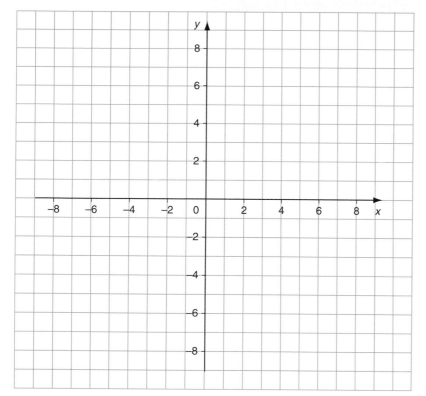

3 **a** Copy and complete this table for the rule $y = 1 - 3x$. Write the set of coordinates produced.

x	−2	−1	0	1	2
$y = 1 - 3x$	7				

b Plot the coordinates on the graph above and label the line correctly.

4 Estimate the coordinates of the intersection of the two lines on the graph.

5 State the gradient and the y intercept of the line for each of these functions:

a $y = 2x + 1$

b $y = -2x - 4$

c $y = 5x$

d $y = x - 3$

How did I do?

	✔
I can plot the graph of a linear function in the form $y = mx + c$.	☐
I can state the gradient and y intercept of a straight-line graph given its function.	☐

Teacher's tips

Whenever $mx = 0$ the line will be horizontal; for the line to be vertical the slope is 'undefined' and the equation is changed to $x = $. The point c is always the point where the line intercepts the y–axis at $x = $ zero.

30: Graphs of functions

You will revise:
▶ graphs of linear and quadratic functions.

 Get started

Functions can be drawn as graphs on a coordinate grid.

Linear functions are those that produce straight lines. They can be written in the form $y = mx + c$, where m and c are numbers.

▶ The **gradient** of the straight line (how steep it is) is the value of m.

▶ The point where the line crosses the y-axis (the y **intercept**) is the value of c.

Quadratic and **cubic** functions produce curved lines, e.g. $y = x^2$, $y = x^3$.

 Practice

1 **a** Copy and complete the table for the function $y = 4x - 3$.

x	−4	−3	−2	−1	0	1	2	3	4
$y = 4x - 3$									

b Plot the pairs of coordinates on a separate sheet of graph paper using the axes shown opposite and label the line correctly.

c What is the gradient of this line?

d What are the coordinates of its y intercept?

 Challenge

2 State the gradient and the y intercept of the line for each of these functions.

a $y = -3x + 5$ **b** $y = 2x - 4$

c $y = -x$ **d** $y = x + 6$

e $y = 5 - x$ **f** $y = 2x - 3$

3 Which two of the functions in question 2:

a are parallel with a positive gradient?

b are parallel with a negative gradient?

c intersect the y axis at the same point?

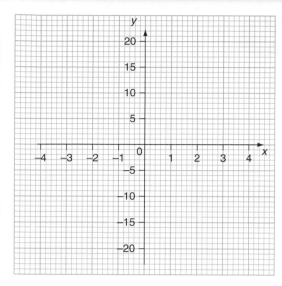

4 **a** Copy and complete this table for the function $y = x^2$.

x	−4	−3	−2	−1	0	1	2	3	4
$y = x^2$									

b Plot the pairs of coordinates on the graph you have drawn earlier. Join the points with a smooth curve.

5 Estimate the coordinates of the two intersections of the two lines on the graph.

6 **a** Copy and complete the table for the function $y = x^2 + 4$.

x	−4	−3	−2	−1	0	1	2	3	4
$y = x^2 + 4$									

b Describe the difference between the graphs of $y = x^2$ and $y = x^2 + 4$.

Try it yourself!

The line $y = 4x$ has a gradient of 4. What is the gradient of a line that is perpendicular to this?

How did I do?

I can plot graphs of linear and quadratic functions.

Teacher's tips

Try plotting graphs for related linear functions (e.g. $y = 5x$, $y = -5x+2$, $y = -5x$), and quadratic functions (e.g. $y = x^2$, $y = x^2 +3$, $y = (x - 4)^2 - 5$), and you will begin to see the relationships between the equation and the shape, gradient, and position of the line/curve.

You will revise:
▶ how to solve problems by first writing a formula.

Get started

Some problems can be solved by writing a formula and substituting values into it. It can help to write the formula in words first and then write it using just symbols, like this:

The length of *P* is four times the length of *R*. So $P = 4R$.

Practice

1 The length of a line AB is *x* cm. The line CD is three times the length of AB. A third line EF is 1 cm longer than CD.

A ————— B
     x

C ————————————— D

E ————————————————— F

a Express the length of line CD in terms of *x*.

b Express the length of line EF in terms of *x*.

c Find the length of CD if line AB is 5 cm long.

d Find the length of EF if line AB is 7 cm long.

Challenge

2 A badge is made from two identical equilateral triangles as shown below. Some of the lengths are shown.

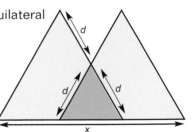

a Write a formula for *x* in terms of *d*.

b Express the perimeter *P* of the badge in terms of *d*.

c Find the length of *x* if *d* = 4 cm.

d Find the perimeter *P* of the badge if *d* = 4 cm.

e Find the value of *d* if the perimeter of the badge is 90 cm.

3   Point C is the centre of a circle with radius, *r*. The circle passes through the centre of the square ABCD. *d* is the shortest distance between the edge of the circle and point D.

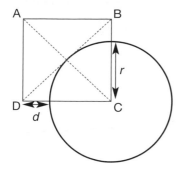

   a Express the length of the diagonal AC in terms of *r*.

   b Express the length of the side AB in terms of *d* and *r*.

   c Express the perimeter *P* of the square ABCD in terms of *d* and *r*.

   d Express the area of the square ABCD in terms of *d* and *r*.

4   Use your answers above to find the following measurements if *d* = 4.1 cm and *r* = 10 cm.

   a The length of the diagonal AC.

   b The length of the side AB.

   c The perimeter *P* of the square ABCD.

   d The area of the square ABCD.

5   The perimeter of a rectangle is 48 cm. Its area is 128 cm². What is the length and width of the rectangle?

How did I do?

I can solve problems by using formulae.   ✔ ☐

Teacher's tips

Make sure that you know the main formulae for finding the dimensions of shapes, as more advanced problems like these will assume that you know them. If you're not sure and diagrams are to scale, measure to check.

You will revise:
- standard metric units for length, mass and capacity
- converting between metric units.

Get started

These diagrams show how to convert from one metric unit to another.

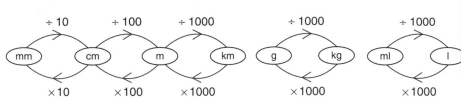

mm ↔ cm	cm ↔ m	m ↔ km	g ↔ kg	ml ↔ l
10 mm = 1 cm	100 cm = 1 m	1000 m = 1 km	1000 g = 1 kg	1000 ml = 1 l

Practice

1   Convert these measurements to the units shown.

a 30 cm = ☐ mm   b 300 cm = ☐ m

c 60 mm = ☐ cm   d 470 mm = ☐ cm

e 9000 m = ☐ km   f 20 000 m = ☐ km

g 5000 mm = ☐ cm   h 700 cm = ☐ mm

i 6 m = ☐ cm   j 400 cm = ☐ mm

k 8000 m = ☐ km   l 700 m = ☐ cm

Challenge

2   Convert these measurements to the units shown.

a 1000 g = ☐ kg   b 7000 g = ☐ kg   c 4500 g = ☐ kg

d 8 kg = ☐ g   e 3.5 kg = ☐ g   f 5.7 kg = ☐ g

g 1.5 l = ☐ ml   h 2500 ml = ☐ l   i 16.8 l = ☐ ml

3 Convert these measurements to the units shown.

a 37 cm = ☐ mm   **b** 128 cm = ☐ m   **c** 67 mm = ☐ cm

d 473 mm = ☐ cm   **e** 986 m = ☐ km   **f** 2380 m = ☐ km

g 4902 m = ☐ km   **h** 354 m = ☐ km   **i** 0.78 m = ☐ cm

4 Convert these measurements to the units shown.

a 1200 g = ☐ kg   **b** 1640 g = ☐ kg   **c** 4362 g = ☐ kg

d 866 g = ☐ kg   **e** 3.5 kg = ☐ g   **f** 5.33 kg = ☐ g

g 1.584 l = ☐ ml   **h** 1647 ml = ☐ l   **i** 16.67 l = ☐ ml

5 Convert these measurements to the units shown.

a 150 mm = ☐ m   **b** 1000 mm = ☐ m   **c** 2500 cm = ☐ km

d 362 mm = ☐ m   **e** 1387 cm = ☐ km   **f** 0.56 m = ☐ mm

g 1560 mm = ☐ m   **h** 8900 cm = ☐ km   **i** 5660 mm = ☐ m

j 8092 mm = ☐ m   **k** 867 cm = ☐ km   **l** 0.819 km = ☐ cm

6 Write whether each statement is true or false:

a 0.007 mm = 7 m   **b** 7 mm = 0.007 m

c 65 cm = 6 500 000 km   **d** 6 500 000 cm = 65 km

e 800 000 mm = 800 m   **f** 800 mm = 800 000 m

g 42 cm = 0.00042 km   **h** 0.000 42 cm = 42 km

7 Arrange these cards to make at least five different pairs of equal measurements. You do not have to use all the cards each time.

| km | m | cm | mm | 6 | 6 | 4 | 4 | 0 | 0 | 0 | 0 |

| . | . | = |

How did I do?

                                   ✔

I know the standard metric units for length, mass and capacity. ☐

I can convert between metric units. ☐

Teacher's tips

The prefixes to measurements help explain what they mean. 'Kilo' means 'a thousand'; 'milli' means 'a thousandth'; centi means 'a hundredth'. So a centimetre is a hundredth of a metre, and there are 100 cm in a metre.

33: Measurement (2)

Get started

Metric units of measurement include:

for length: millimetres, centimetres, metres and kilometres;
for mass: grams and kilograms;
for capacity: millilitres, centilitres and litres.

To convert one metric unit to another you multiply by 10, 100, 1000 or some other power of 10, using these equivalents:

10 mm = 1 cm, 100 cm = 1 m, 1000 m = 1 km
1000 g = 1 kg
10 ml = 1 cl, 100 cl = 1 l

Imperial units of measurement include:

for length: inches, feet, yards and miles;
for mass: ounces, pounds and stones;
for capacity: pints and gallons.

To convert one metric unit to an imperial unit or vice versa, use approximate equivalents, such as 1 kg ≈ 2.2 pounds.

Practice

1 Convert these metric measurements to the units shown.

a 54 cm = ☐ mm	**b** 162 cm = ☐ m	**c** 58 mm = ☐ cm
d 267 mm = ☐ cm	**e** 1700 m = ☐ km	**f** 1850 m = ☐ km
g 7202 m = ☐ km	**h** 877 m = ☐ km	**i** 0.51 m = ☐ cm
j 1700 g = ☐ kg	**k** 1960 g = ☐ kg	**l** 4082 g = ☐ kg
m 834 g = ☐ kg	**n** 9.5 kg = ☐ g	**o** 5.21 kg = ☐ g
p 1.876 l = ☐ ml	**q** 1218 ml = ☐ l	**r** 24.67 l = ☐ ml

Challenge

2 Use the approximate equivalents in the table to convert these imperial measurements to metric units.

Imperial to metric: length
1 inch ≈ 2.54 cm
1 foot ≈ 30 cm
1 yard ≈ 91 cm
1 mile ≈ 1.6 km

a 12 inches ≈ ☐ cm **b** 3 yards ≈ ☐ cm **c** 5 miles ≈ ☐ km

d 6 inches ≈ ☐ cm **e** 3500 yards ≈ ☐ cm **f** 2 miles ≈ ☐ m

3 Use the approximate equivalents in the table to convert these metric measurements to imperial units. You may use a calculator.

> **Metric to imperial: length**
> 1 cm ≈ 0.4 inches
> 1 m ≈ 3.3 feet
> 1 m ≈ 1.1 yards
> 1 km ≈ 0.62 miles

a 12 cm ≈ ☐ inches **b** 150 km ≈ ☐ miles **c** 3 m ≈ ☐ feet

d 294 km ≈ ☐ miles **e** 6 m ≈ ☐ yards **f** 60 m ≈ ☐ yards

g 21 m ≈ ☐ feet **h** 0.06 m ≈ ☐ inches

4 Convert these metric measurements to the units shown. You may use a calculator.

a 8340 mm = ☐ m **b** 95 000 mm = ☐ km

c 5210 cm = ☐ km **d** 18.76 m = ☐ mm

e 1.218 km = ☐ cm **f** 0.2467 km = ☐ mm

5 Use the approximate equivalents in the table to convert these metric measurements to imperial units and vice versa. You may use a calculator.

Imperial to metric: mass	Metric to imperial: mass
1 ounce ≈ 28 g	1 g ≈ 0.035 ounces
1 pound ≈ 454 g	1 kg ≈ 2.2 pounds
1 stone ≈ 6.35 kg	1 kg ≈ 0.16 stones
Imperial to metric: capacity	**Metric to imperial: capacity**
1 pint ≈ 568 ml	1 l ≈ 1.75 pints
1 gallon ≈ 4.55 l	1 l ≈ 0.22 gallons

a 120 g ≈ ☐ ounces **b** 4 ounces ≈ ☐ g

c 3 pounds ≈ ☐ g **d** 19 pounds ≈ ☐ kg

e 18 kg ≈ ☐ pounds **f** 5 stone ≈ ☐ kg

g 21 kg ≈ ☐ stone **h** 600 g ≈ ☐ stone

i 8 pints ≈ ☐ ml **j** 4.5 l ≈ ☐ pints

k 9 gallons ≈ ☐ l **l** 24 l ≈ ☐ gallons

m 1800 g ≈ ☐ stone **n** 0.4 stone ≈ ☐ g

o 6.6 pints ≈ ☐ l **p** 8500 ml ≈ ☐ pints

q 0.2 gallons ≈ ☐ ml **r** 4500 ml ≈ ☐ gallons

How did I do?

	✔
I know metric and imperial units for length, mass and capacity.	☐
I can convert between metric and imperial units.	☐

Teacher's tips

Learn some everyday comparisons between metric and imperial measurements to help check that answers make sense. For instance, a 30 cm ruler is approximately 12 inches (or 1 foot), 1 mile is 1.6 km and a 1 litre bottle of drink is 1¾ pints.

34: Constructing triangles

You will revise:

▶ using a ruler and protractor to construct triangles from given information.

 Get started

You will need a protractor, a ruler and a sharp pencil.

Protractors are used to measure and draw angles. They can be semicircular or circular.

When drawing angles, make sure the central cross of the protractor is at the end of the line where the angle will be and that the line matches up with the zero line on the protractor.

 Practice

1 Here is a triangle ABC.

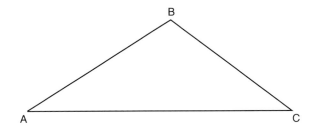

a Use a ruler to measure side AC in centimetres.

b Use a protractor to measure angle A.

c Use a ruler to measure side AB in centimetres.

 Challenge

2 Use a ruler and protractor to construct triangle ABC with:

side AC = 5 cm, angle A = 58°, side AB = 4 cm

Now measure the length of side BC.

3 Use a ruler and protractor to construct triangle ABC with:

side AC = 4.2 cm, angle A = 23°, side AB = 4.3 cm

Now measure the length of side BC.

4 Here is a triangle ABC.

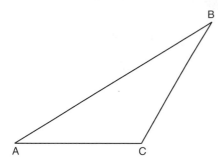

    a Use a protractor to measure angle A.

    b Use a ruler to measure side AC in centimetres.

    c Use a protractor to measure angle C.

5 Use a ruler and a protractor to construct triangle ABC with:

angle A = 44°, side AC = 7 cm, angle C = 67°

    a Measure angle B.

    b Measure the length of side AB.

    c Measure the length of side BC.

6 Use a ruler and a protractor to construct a triangle ABC with:

angle A = 24°, side AC = 6.6 cm, angle C = 98°

    a Measure angle B.

    b Measure the length of side AB.

    c Measure the length of side BC.

7 Match these triangles to their correct descriptions.

Triangle 1: angle A = 30°, angle B = 60°, angle C = 90°

Triangle 2: angle A = 30°, angle B = 80°, angle C = 70°

Triangle 3: angle A = 110°, side AB = side AC

scalene triangle	obtuse isosceles triangle

right-angled scalene triangle

How did I do?

I can use a ruler and protractor to construct triangles from given information.

You will revise:

▶ standard constructions using straight edge and compasses.

Get started

You will need compasses, a ruler and a sharp pencil.

The edge of a circle is always the same distance from its centre. So if you set compasses to a particular length and draw part of a circle, each point on the curved line that you have drawn will be the same length from where the compass point was. When constructing shapes, compasses can be used to find possible positions for the vertices of shapes.

To construct the **perpendicular bisector of a line** means to draw another line at right angles to it exactly in the middle.

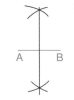

Use compasses to mark parts of circles with the same radius each time. Join their intersections to show the perpendicular bisector.

Practice

1 Use compasses and a ruler to construct an equilateral triangle with sides of 7 cm. Label the triangle ABC.

Challenge

Try it yourself!

Explain how the constructions on these two pages show that the diagonals of a rhombus are perpendicular to each other.

2 Draw lines like these. Construct the perpendicular bisector of each line.

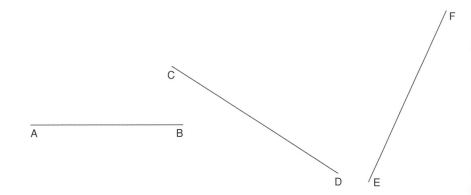

3 To construct the **bisector of an angle**, draw part of a circle with its centre at the corner of the angle. Then draw parts of circles with the same radius, placing the point of the compasses on the side of each line of the angle where the first circle crosses.

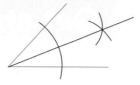

Draw angles like these (they don't need to be exact copies). Construct the bisector of each angle.

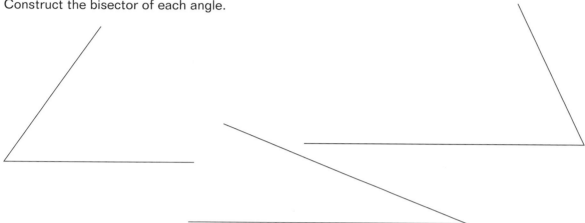

4 To construct the **perpendicular from a point P on a line**, first mark two points on the line equidistant from P using compasses. Draw four more arcs from these two points.

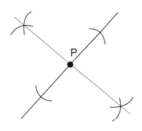

Draw lines like these and mark a point P on each of them (they don't have to be exact copies). Construct the perpendicular from the point P on each line.

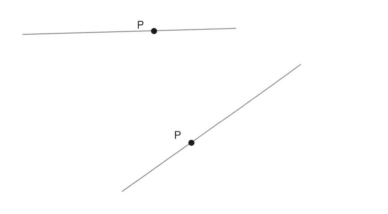

How did I do?

	✔
I can construct the perpendicular bisector of a line.	☐
I can construct the bisector of an angle.	☐
I can construct the perpendicular from a point on a line.	☐

Teacher's tips

It's important that each part of the circle has the same radius for these methods to work. Make sure the compass doesn't get bigger or smaller when you're using it, and fix the pencil securely so that it doesn't slip.

You will revise:
- the perimeter and area of shapes
- how to find the perimeter and area of a shape, including using formulae.

Get started

Perimeter is the distance around the edge of a shape. It is measured in units of length such as centimetres (cm) or metres (m).

The perimeter P of a rectangle of length l and width w can be found using the formula $P = 2(l + w)$.

Area is the amount of surface that a shape covers. It is the space inside the outline of a 2-D shape or within a boundary. Area is measured in square units such as square centimetres (cm^2) or square metres (m^2).

The area A of a rectangle can be found using the formula $A = l \times w$.

Practice

1 Find the perimeter and area of this rectangle. Give the correct unit of measurement.

7 cm

This is not drawn to scale.

3 cm

2 Find the perimeter and area of this rectangle. Give the correct unit of measurement.

7.5 cm

This is not drawn to scale.

4 cm

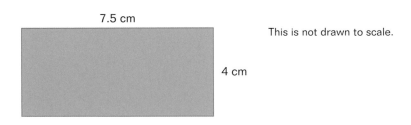

Challenge

3 Find the perimeter and area of each shape by splitting it into rectangles, giving the correct unit of measurement.

a

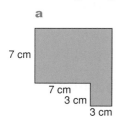

7 cm
7 cm
3 cm
3 cm

b

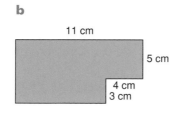

11 cm
5 cm
4 cm
3 cm

c

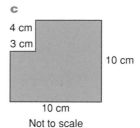

4 cm
3 cm
10 cm
10 cm

Not to scale

4 Find the perimeter and area of each shape by splitting it into rectangles, giving the correct unit of measurement.

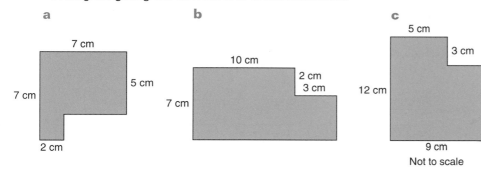

a

7 cm
7 cm
5 cm
2 cm

b

10 cm
2 cm
3 cm
7 cm

c

5 cm
3 cm
12 cm
9 cm

Not to scale

5 Find the perimeter and area of each shape by splitting it into rectangles, giving the correct unit of measurement.

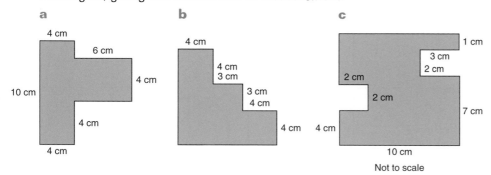

a

4 cm
6 cm
4 cm
10 cm
4 cm
4 cm

b

4 cm
4 cm
3 cm
3 cm
4 cm
4 cm

c

1 cm
3 cm
2 cm
2 cm
2 cm
7 cm
4 cm
10 cm

Not to scale

Try it yourself!

A rectangle has an area of 48 cm². Its length is 2 cm longer than its width. What is the perimeter of the rectangle?

How did I do?

I can find the perimeter and area of a shape, including using formulae.

Teacher's tips

Use a ruler to draw new lines when splitting irregular shapes into more than one rectangle. Note the length of each new side next to it, remembering to use the length of the parallel lines to help calculate unknown lengths.

You will revise:
- the naming of parts of a circle
- finding the area and circumference of a circle.

Get started

A circle is a set of points all the same distance from its centre.

The **circumference** of a circle is found by multiplying the diameter by pi, π.

$$\text{Circumference} = \pi \times d \quad \text{or} \quad \text{Circumference} = \pi \times r \times 2$$

The **area** of a circle is found by squaring the radius and multiplying by π. This can be written as:

$$\text{Area of circle} = \pi \times r \times r \quad \text{or} \quad \text{Area of circle} = \pi r^2$$

Practice

1 Each circle diagram below has a part that is shaded or in bold. Which of these labels goes with each diagram?

| circumference | major arc | semicircle | minor arc |

| radius | diameter | tangent | segment | major sector |

| chord | minor sector |

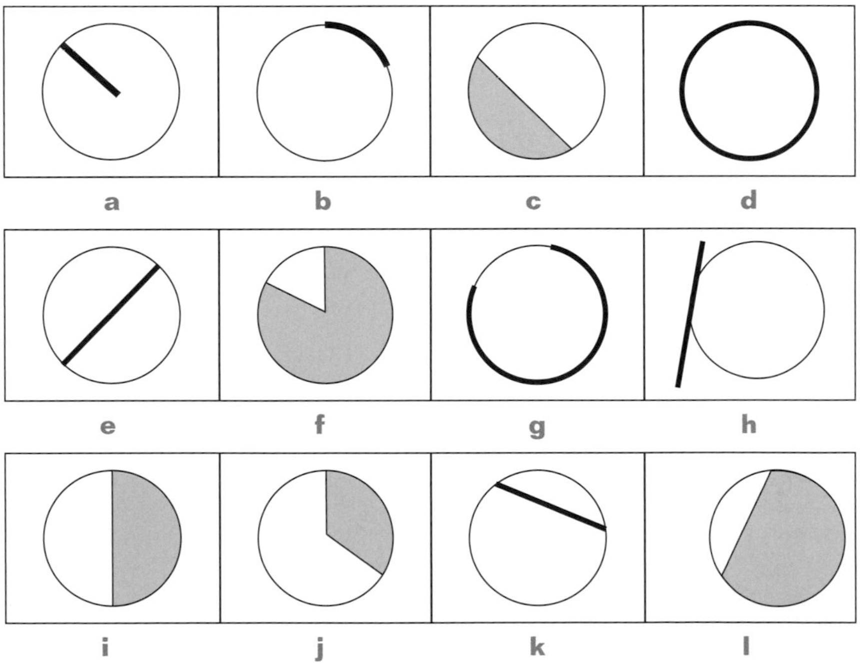

a   b   c   d

e   f   g   h

i   j   k   l

Challenge

2 Find the circumference of each circle using the π key on your calculator. Round your answers to 2 d.p.

a 3.2 cm

b 8.6 cm

c 4.7 cm

d 2.9 cm

3 Find the area of each circle using the x^2 and π keys on your calculator. Round your answers to 2 d.p.

a 5 cm

b 7.2 cm

c 11.5 cm

d 12.6 cm

4 A jewellery shop makes brooches made from wire. Find the amount of wire used for each of these brooches. They are not drawn to scale. Give your answers to 2 d.p.

a Each diameter is 1.5 cm.

b The larger circle has a diameter of 5 cm.

c The larger circle has a diameter of 4 cm.

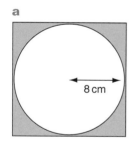
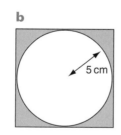

5 Find the area of each shaded part of these shapes. Give your answers to 2 d.p.

a

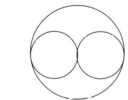
8 cm

b

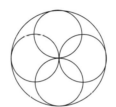
5 cm

c

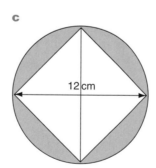
12 cm

Teacher's tips

The x^2 button on a calculator simply means 'squared' so it works for r^2 as well. For questions 4 and 5 it will help to sketch the lines that you need (diameter, radius) with their measurements, before applying the appropriate formulae.

You will revise:

▶ how to find the surface area of a cuboid.

Get started

Area is the amount of surface that a shape covers. In a 2-D shape (flat shape) it is the space inside the lines or within a boundary. In a 3-D shape (solid shape) it is the total amount of surface of all the faces. For 3-D shapes this is often called the **surface area**.

Surface area is measured in square units such as square centimetres (cm²) or square metres (m²).

Practice

1 Find the missing dimensions on the net of this cuboid.

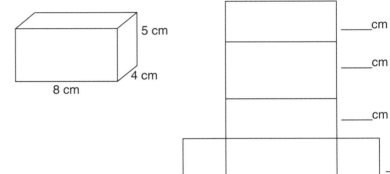

Not to scale

Work out the area of each rectangle of the net and use your answers to find the cuboid's surface area.

Challenge

2 Find the surface area of this cuboid. Sketch a net to help you.

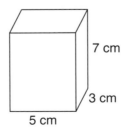

Not to scale

3 Find the surface area of this cuboid. Sketch a net to help you.

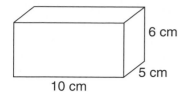

6 cm

5 cm

10 cm

Not to scale

4 The formula for the surface area *S* of a cuboid with length *l*, breadth *b* and height *h* is:

$S = 2bl + 2lh + 2hb$

Find the surface area for a cuboid with these dimensions.

a *l* = 7 cm, *b* = 5 cm, *h* = 12 cm   **b** *l* = 9 cm, *b* = 4 cm, *h* = 6 cm

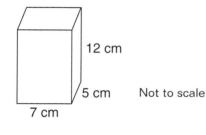

12 cm

5 cm   Not to scale

7 cm

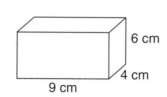

6 cm

4 cm

9 cm

c *l* = 4 cm, *b* = 2 cm, *h* = 8 cm   **d** *l* = 15 cm, *b* − 7 cm, *h* = 6 cm

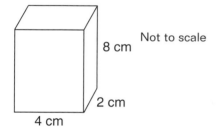

8 cm

Not to scale

2 cm

4 cm

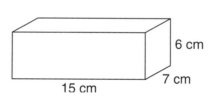

6 cm

7 cm

15 cm

5 A cuboid has a length of 6 cm and a width of 4 cm. What is its height if its surface area is 148 cm²?

Teacher's tips

An alternative to drawing a net is to calculate the area of each of the 3 faces in the diagram (writing answers on the faces as you go), add them up, and then double the answer (to include the 3 faces not shown).

You will revise:

▶ the surface area and volume of cuboids and shapes based on cuboids.

Get started

Area is the amount of surface that a shape covers. In a 2-D shape (flat shape) it is the space inside the lines or within a boundary. In a 3-D shape (solid shape) it is the total amount of surface of all the faces. For 3-D shapes this is often called the **surface area**. Surface area is measured in square units like square centimetres (cm^2) or square metres (m^2).

To find the surface area S of a cuboid, use the formula $S = 2bl + 2hl + 2hb$, where l is the cuboid's length, b its breadth and h its height.

Volume is the space inside a 3-D shape. It is measured in cubic millimetres (mm^3), cubic centimetres (cm^3) and cubic metres (m^3).

To find the volume V of a cuboid use the formula $V = lbh$, where l is the cuboid's length, b its breadth and h its height.

Practice

1 Use the formula $V = lbh$ to find the volume of each box.

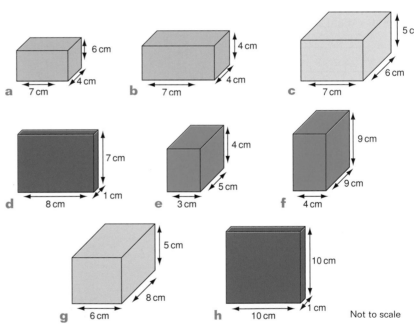

Challenge

2 Use the formula $S = 2bl + 2hl + 2hb$ to find the surface area of each of the cuboids above.

3 Copy and complete this table.

Box	Dimensions			Volume (cm³) $V = lbh$	Surface area (cm²) $S = 2bl + 2hl + 2hb$
	l	b	h		
A	6 cm	2 cm	5 cm		
B	8 cm	4 cm	2 cm		
C	9 cm	3 cm	8 cm		
D	7 cm	3 cm	10 cm		
E	6 cm	2 cm	6 cm		
F	9 cm	4 cm	7 cm		

4 Calculate **i** the volume and **ii** the surface area of each triangular prism. Each triangle is right-angled.

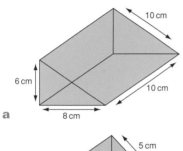

a

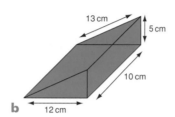

b

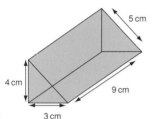

c

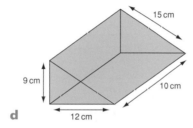

d

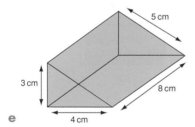

e

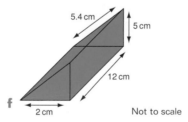

f

Not to scale

5 A cuboid has a surface area of 94 cm². Its length is 4 cm larger than its width and 2 cm smaller than its height. What is the volume of the cuboid?

Teacher's tips

The area of a triangle is: ½ x base x height. The volume of a prism is the area of the triangular face x length. This formula of: area of the face x length works for the volume of all prisms.

40: Volume

You will revise:
- using formulae to find the volume of cuboids, prisms and cylinders.

Get started

Volume is the space inside a 3-D shape. It is measured in cubic millimetres (mm³), cubic centimetres (cm³) and cubic metres (m³).

To find the volume V of a cuboid use the formula **$V = lbh$**, where l is the cuboid's length, b its breadth and h its height.

A **prism** is a 3-D shape that has the same cross-section all the way along its length.

To find the volume of a prism, first find the area of the end face, then multiply by the length of the prism.

If finding the volume of a **cylinder**, find the area of the end face using the formula $A = \pi r^2$, where r is the radius of the circle.

Practice

1. Use the formula $V = lbh$ to find the volume of each box.

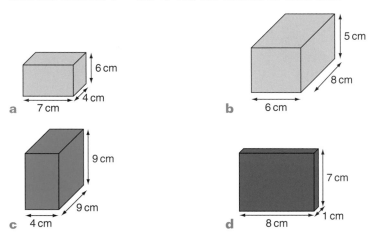

a 7 cm 6 cm 4 cm

b 6 cm 5 cm 8 cm

c 4 cm 9 cm 9 cm

d 8 cm 7 cm 1 cm

Challenge

2. Calculate the volume of each shape, given the area of the end face.

a   b   c   d

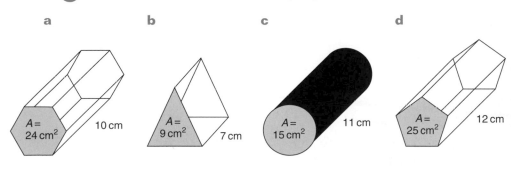

a $A = 24\,cm^2$ 10 cm

b $A = 9\,cm^2$ 7 cm

c $A = 15\,cm^2$ 11 cm

d $A = 25\,cm^2$ 12 cm

3 Calculate the volume of each triangular prism. Each triangle is right angled.

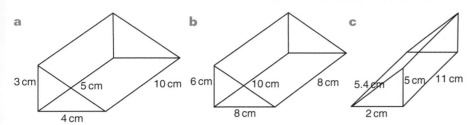

a

3 cm 5 cm 10 cm

4 cm

b

6 cm 10 cm 8 cm

8 cm

c

5.4 cm 5 cm 11 cm

2 cm

4 Calculate the volume of each triangular prism. The triangles are not right angled. The perpendicular heights are given in red.

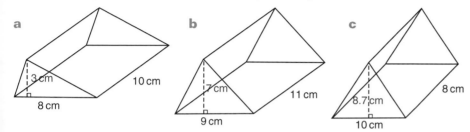

a

3 cm 10 cm

8 cm

b

7 cm 11 cm

9 cm

c

8.7 cm 8 cm

10 cm

5 Calculate the volume of each cylinder, given its radius. Give your answers to the nearest cm³.

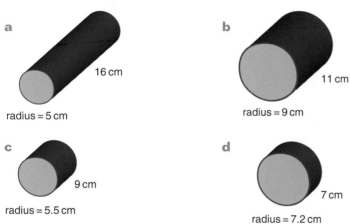

a

16 cm

radius = 5 cm

b

11 cm

radius = 9 cm

c

9 cm

radius = 5.5 cm

d

7 cm

radius = 7.2 cm

Try it yourself!

A coin lying on a table has a height of 2 mm and a diameter of 2.5 cm. Find its volume in mm³ to the nearest whole number.

How did I do?

I can calculate the volume of cuboids, prisms and cylinders. ✔

Teacher's tips

The most common mistakes when calculating volume and surface area are to either apply the wrong formula, or express the answer in the wrong units (squared or cubed) – so take time to check both carefully!

41: Angles (1)

You will revise:

▸ the properties of angles and parallel lines

▸ using these properties to solve problems.

Get started

Angles on a straight line add up to 180°. Angles around a point add up to 360°.

The sum of the interior angles of a triangle is 180°. The sum of the interior angles of a quadrilateral is 360°.

When a straight line crosses two parallel lines, some equal angles are formed.

The angles in an F-shape are equal. These are called **corresponding angles**.

The angles in a Z-shape are equal. These are called **alternate angles**.

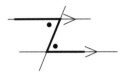

Practice

1 Use the sum of the interior angles of a quadrilateral, a triangle or a straight line to help you calculate the size of each of the marked angles:

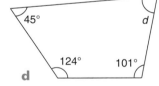
a

b

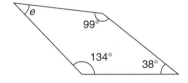
c

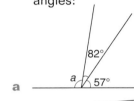

Not to scale d

e

Challenge

2 Copy each diagram. Label every angle in your copy with its size.

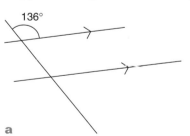
a

Not to scale

b

3 Find the size of each angle.

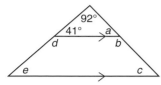

Not to scale

4 Find the size of each angle.

Not to scale

5 Find the size of each angle.

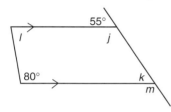

Not to scale

6 Find the value of each angle marked by a letter.

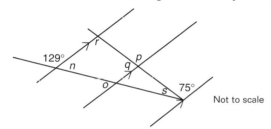

Not to scale

7 Find the value of each angle marked by a letter.

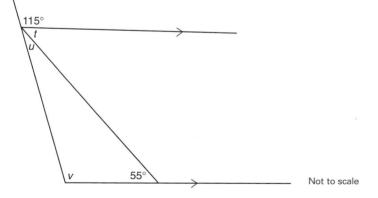

Not to scale

Teacher's tips

You may not have sufficient information to calculate the final answer immediately, so think about what you can calculate using the facts you know. Follow a trail; find one unknown angle and that answer helps you find the next.

You will revise:
▶ the properties of interior and exterior angles of regular and irregular polygons.

Get started

To find the sum of the **interior angles** of a polygon, imagine splitting the shape into triangles from just one corner. The number of triangles is always 2 fewer than the number of sides of the shape, so if a shape has 24 sides it would have 22 triangles.

Because you know that the sum of the angles of a triangle is 180°, multiply the number of triangles by 180° to find the sum of all the angles in the shape. This can be shown in the formula:

Sum of the interior angles = $180(n - 2)$, where n is the number of sides.

For regular shapes, once the sum of the interior angles is known, each angle can be found. Divide the sum of the interior angles by the number of sides.

Remember also that the sum of the **exterior angles** of any polygon always add up to 360°.

Practice

1 Find the sum of the interior angles of each polygon.

a hexagon   **b** decagon   **c** pentagon

d nonagon   **e** heptagon   **f** dodecagon (12 sides)

Challenge

2 Find the size of each angle in the regular polygons below. You can use a calculator. Give answers to the nearest degree.

a regular octagon   **b** regular heptagon   **c** regular hexagon

d regular decagon   **e** regular nonagon   **f** regular pentagon

3 Sketch this diagram. Label your sketch with the size of each interior and exterior angle. Find the missing angle, *a*.

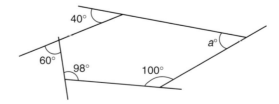

4 A regular shape has 28 sides. Find the size of one of its interior angles (to the nearest degree).

5 A regular shape has equal interior angles that are 168°. How many sides has the shape?

6 A regular shape has equal exterior angles. Each is 18°. How many sides has the shape?

7 An irregular shape has interior angles with the sum of 2880°. How many sides has the shape?

8 An irregular pentagon has exterior angles of 24°, 45°, 130°, 100° and $x°$. Find the value of x. List all the interior angles of the pentagon.

9 An irregular octagon has interior angles of 142°, 13°, 250°, 37°, 328°, 15°, 20° and $x°$. Find the value of x.

10 What is the size difference between the sum of the interior angles of a decagon and the sum of the exterior angles of a decagon?

11 a Find the value of x in each of these irregular polygons.

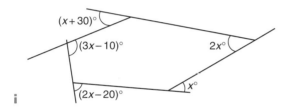

i

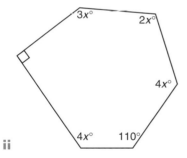

ii

b Find the sizes of the interior angles in each polygon.

Teacher's tips

Use the same technique as in Unit 41 to find the unknown interior angles in a polygon, except this time you have an extra 'clue' to use (that the sum of the interior angles $= 180(n-2)$ where $n=$ number of sides).

You will revise:

▶ transforming 2-D shapes using reflection, translation, rotation and enlargement.

Get started

Transformations are ways of changing or moving shapes. There are several transformations you should know about: **reflection**, **rotation**, **translation** and **enlargement**. As a shape is changed, the new shape is called the **image**.

▶ To **reflect** a shape you need a mirror line. Mirror lines can be horizontal, vertical or diagonal.

▶ **Translation** just means a move or slide without turning. A translation can be vertical, horizontal or diagonal.

▶ A **rotation** means a turn. To rotate a shape you need a centre of rotation. You also need to know through what angle and direction you are rotating the shape.

▶ An **enlargement** of a shape changes the size of it. An enlargement of a scale factor 2 makes every side of the shape twice as long. An enlargement of a scale factor 3 makes every side of the shape three times as long and so on.

Practice

1 Measure some of the lengths of the sides of shapes A, B, C and D. Use the measurements to help you state the scale factor of enlargement that maps:

a A onto B   **b** A onto C   **c** A onto D   **d** B onto D

 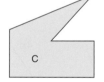 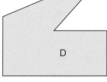

Challenge

2 Copy these shapes onto grid paper. Reflect each shape below in the x-axis. The shapes will overlap and the outline of them together forms a polygon. Name the polygon. One has been done for you.

  a   **b**   **c**   **d**

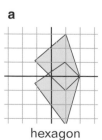 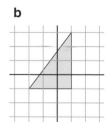 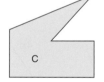 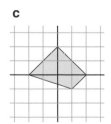 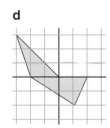

hexagon

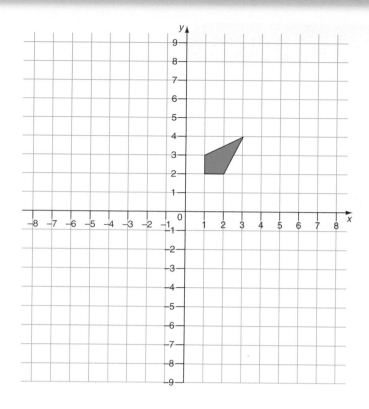

3. Copy the blue shape above onto grid paper. Transform the shape in different ways as described below and label each image.

    a. Enlarge the shape by scale factor 2 with centre of enlargement at (0, 0) to make image A.

    b. Rotate the shape clockwise through 90° about the point (0, 0) to make image B.

    c. Reflect the shape in the line $y = -2$ to make image C.

    d. Reflect the shape in the line $x = -1$ to make image D.

    e. Enlarge the shape by scale factor 3 with centre of enlargement at (5, 6) to make image E.

Try it yourself!

Which single transformation is the same as a reflection in the line $x = y$, followed by a reflection in the x-axis?

How did I do?

I can transform 2-D shapes using reflection, translation, rotation and enlargement. ✔ ☐

Teacher's tips

To enlarge a shape with centre of enlargement (COE), draw guidelines from the COE to each corner of the shape. Extend these lines by the factor of enlargement, then join the points of each line to make the new shape.

You will revise:

▶ how to investigate and solve shape and space problems.

Get started

When solving problems or investigating mathematical situations, it is often easier to break the problem down into smaller steps and then to look for patterns. Breaking it into smaller steps might mean starting with a smaller number and working your way up systematically. Drawing and completing a table can also help you to analyse the information more clearly.

Practice

1 This design has three different-sized squares: small, medium and the large square itself. Find the total number of squares in the design.

2 This design has three different-sized triangles: small, medium and the large triangle itself. Find the total number of triangles in the design.

Challenge

3 You can split a square into 3 regions using 2 straight lines, like this:

Or you can use 2 straight lines to split the square into 4 regions, like this:

Find the smallest number of straight lines needed to create:

a 6 regions

b 9 regions

c Copy and complete this table.

Number of lines	0	1	2	3	4	5	6
Maximum number of regions							

4 Investigate the number of squares in each shape. Remember to include different-sized squares. Copy and fill in the table. Look for patterns and see if you can predict the number of squares in the next shape of the sequence.

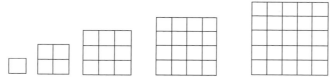

1 × 1 squares	1	4		
2 × 2 squares	0	1		
3 × 3 squares	0	0		
4 × 4 squares	0	0		
5 × 5 squares	0	0		

Try it yourself!

Is it possible to have a triangle with two obtuse angles? Explain your answer.

5 Investigate the number of cubes in each shape. Remember to include different sized cubes. Copy and fill in the table. Look for patterns and see if you can predict the number of cubes in the next shape of the sequence.

1 × 1 × 1 cubes	1
2 × 2 × 2 cubes	0
3 × 3 × 3 cubes	0
4 × 4 × 4 cubes	0
Total number of cubes	1

6 Investigate the total number of triangles in this design.

How did I do?

I can investigate and solve shape and space problems.

Teacher's tips

Once you've completed the table you might be able to see a pattern and then express the relationship as an equation. This formula can then be used to solve much more complex problems (e.g. bigger shapes).

You will revise:

▶ finding the midpoint of a line segment given its end points

▶ using Pythagoras' theorem to calculate lengths.

 Get started

The **midpoint** of a line is the point exactly in the middle of it.

If the end points of the line have the coordinates (x_1, y_1) and (x_2, y_2), these formulae can be used:

▶ the x-coordinate of the midpoint is $\frac{1}{2}(x_1 + x_2)$

▶ the y-coordinate of the midpoint is $\frac{1}{2}(y_1 + y_2)$.

The length of the hypotenuse (the longest side) of a right-angled triangle can be found using **Pythagoras' theorem**:

▶ the hypotenuse squared is equal to the sum of the squares of the two shorter sides.

Pythagoras' theorem can be written as:

$c^2 = a^2 + b^2$ or $c = \sqrt{(a^2 + b^2)}$

where c is the hypotenuse and a and b are the shorter sides.

 Practice

1 Find the coordinates of the midpoint M of the line PQ if the coordinates of P and Q are as follows.

a P (4, 6) and Q (2, 0)   **b** P (2, 7) and Q (8, 1)

c P (−3, −4) and Q (−1, −2)   **d** P (0, −3) and Q (−4, −5)

e P (−7, −2) and Q (1, 4)   **f** P (−6, 5) and Q (8, −1)

g P (1, −2) and Q (6, −6)   **h** P (−4, 5) and Q (0, 8)

i P (−3, 9) and Q (5, −4)   **j** P (−8, −3) and Q (1, −6)

2 Check your answers by plotting the pairs of points P and Q and finding their midpoints on grid paper using the axes shown here.

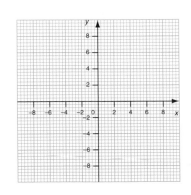

Challenge

3 Use Pythagoras' theorem to find the hypotenuse of each right-angled triangle. Use the √ key on your calculator. Round your answers to 1 decimal place.

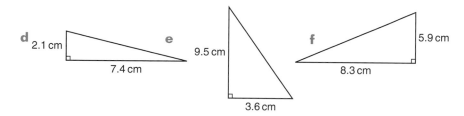

4 Copy the axes below onto grid paper. For each part, plot the points P and Q on the grid and join them with a line. Draw a vertical and horizontal line to make a right-angled triangle with the hypotenuse PQ. Find the lengths of the other two sides of the triangle using the coordinates of P and Q. Now use Pythagoras' theorem to find the length of the line PQ to 1 d.p. Do not use a ruler for this question.

a P (0, 0) and Q (3, 4)   **b** P (1, 4) and Q (5, 6)

c P (−1, −1) and Q (−3, −5)   **d** P (−3, 2) and Q (5, −4)

e P (0, −2) and Q (−3, 5)

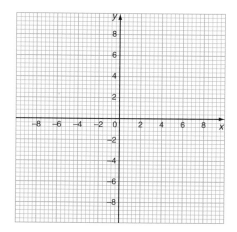

How did I do?

✔

I can find the midpoint of a line segment given its end points. ☐

I can use Pythagoras' theorem to calculate lengths. ☐

Teacher's tips

Pythagoras' theorem works with BODMAS in exactly the same way as any other formula. Remember that the 'O' in BODMAS means 'other' and includes squares and square roots. In this case calculate the squares first as they are in brackets.

46: Statistics

Get started

Averages are used to represent a middle or typical value in a set of numbers. There are three types of average: mean, median and mode.

▶ To find the **mode**, look for the most popular, or frequent, value or values in the list or table.

▶ To find the **median**, put all the values in order and then find the middle value. If there are two middle values then the median is the number halfway between them.

▶ To find the **mean**, find the total of all the values and then divide this by the number of values.

▶ To find the mean when the data is in a table, multiply each value by the frequency and find the total. Then divide by the total frequency.

The **range** is the difference between the highest and lowest values.

Practice

1 Find the mode, median, range and mean of this set of data. You may use a calculator. Round your answers to 1 d.p.

12, 15, 8, 12, 17, 21, 15, 22, 16, 36, 29, 18, 12

Challenge

2 Copy and complete the table to find the mean of this set of data. You may use a calculator. Round answers to two decimal places. Then state the mode.

Score (s)	Frequency (f)	$s \times f$
4	3	
5	2	
6	9	
7	4	
8	6	
9	1	
Totals		

Mean = ____ Mode = ____

3 Find the mean of these 14 numbers.

269, 427, 841, 17, 261, 814, 32, 231, 360, 514, 26, 717, 391, 420

4 A class of 30 students had a mean score of 48 in an exam. Another class of 24 had a mean of 52.5. What was the mean for all 54 students?

5 A travel agent sold a mean of 5.4 holidays an hour over 16 hours. During the following 24 hours it sold a mean of 7.2. What was the mean over the whole period?

6 A student has a mean score of 72% from 8 tests. She has 1 more test to go and wants a mean score of 75%. What % will she need to get in her final test?

7 The mean of the information in this table is exactly 18. A number has been left out of the table. What is that number?

Number	16	17	18	19	20
Frequency	46	38	15	32	. . .

8 A netball team had a mean score of 28 in its first 12 matches. In its next 8 matches their mean was 33. What was the mean for all 20 matches?

9 This table gives information about the size of classes in Eskdale School. Copy and complete the table and then find the mean, median and mode of the number of pupils per class at the school.

Number of pupils per class	Number of classes	Number of pupils
25	1	
26	0	
27	7	
28	6	
29	8	
30	2	
31	3	
32	1	
33+	0	
Totals		

Teacher's tips

First, rewrite sets of data so values are arranged in numerical order to make calculating median, mode and range easier. It can also be useful to write each value out, when it occurs more than once, to find the median.

You will revise:
- drawing and interpreting pie charts.

Get started

To find the angle of each sector of a **pie chart**, find the fraction of the whole (of 360°) that each section represents. This can be done by adding extra columns to the table. In the table below, the total number of boys is 100, so this is the denominator of each fraction. It is multiplied by 360° to find the angle of the sector. The angles are rounded to the nearest degree.

Activity or item	Number of boys	Calculation (fraction × 360)	Angle of sector
Sports and hobbies	45	$\frac{45}{100} \times 360$	162°
Going out	10	$\frac{10}{100} \times 360$	36°
CDs, videos, DVDs	18	$\frac{18}{100} \times 360$	64.8 → 65°
Clothes	9	$\frac{9}{100} \times 360$	32.4 → 32°
Computer games	11	$\frac{11}{100} \times 360$	39.6 → 40°
Other	7	$\frac{7}{100} \times 360$	25.2 → 25°

Practice

1. In a survey of 240 people, 128 were female.

   a What fraction of the whole group were female?

   b If the group of 240 people were shown in a pie chart, what would be the size of the sector for 'females' in degrees?

Challenge

2. Copy and complete both tables.

Table 1: Which flavour crisps are preferred by 80 thirteen-year-old girls?

Flavour	Frequency	Calculation (fraction × 360)	Angle of sector
Cheese and onion	23		
Prawn cocktail	13		
Ready salted	4		
Salt and vinegar	11		
Smoky bacon	21		
Other	8		

Table 2: Which flavour crisps are preferred by 110 thirteen-year-old boys?

Flavour	Frequency	Calculation (fraction × 360)	Angle of sector
Cheese and onion	31		
Prawn cocktail	8		
Ready salted	5		
Salt and vinegar	28		
Smoky bacon	21		
Other	17		

3 In your notebook, now draw two pie charts of the data in the two tables, using the same colours for the sectors in both pie charts. Give each pie chart a title and label or provide a key for each sector.

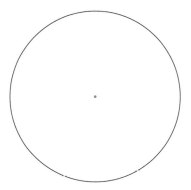 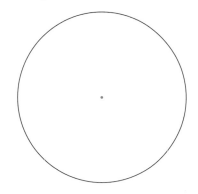

4 Compare the two pie charts and write three statements about differences between the favourite flavours of crisps of the thirteen-year-old boys and girls.

Try it yourself!

A pie chart shows the results of a survey asking 7200 people to state their favourite colour. One sector of the pie is 64°, showing how many people's favourite colour was blue. How many people chose blue as their favourite colour?

How did I do?

I can draw and interpret pie charts.

Teacher's tips

When expressing data as fractions, the total in a set is always the denominator, each part is the numerator (and the total of the numerators equals the denominator). To compare different data sets a common denominator is found (and fractions simplified).

You will revise:

▶ scatter graphs, correlation and lines of best fit.

Get started

Scatter graphs show whether there is a connection between two sets of values. A connection could show:

▶ that one value increases as the other increases (**positive correlation**)

▶ that one value increases as the other decreases (**negative correlation**)

▶ no connection at all (**zero correlation**).

If there is a correlation between two things, a **line of best fit** can be drawn. This is a line that best represents the data on the graph. The line of best fit can be used to help predict or estimate other information.

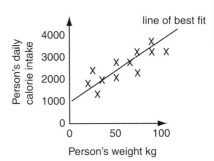

Practice

1 Do these scatter graphs show positive, negative or zero correlation?

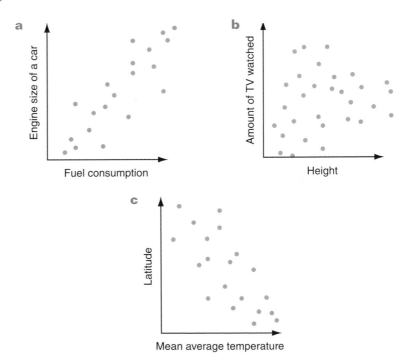

Challenge

2 Copy the axes below onto grid paper. Use the data in this table to complete the scatter diagram below. The data show the heights and weights of 10 women.

Height (cm)	148	158	163	138	142	169	132	171	152	155
Weight (kg)	55	67	68	58	53	72	47	76	59	64

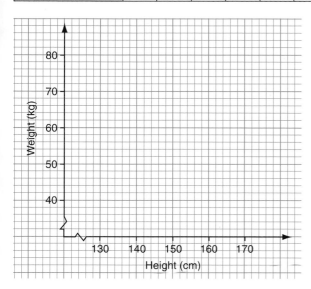

3 State what type of correlation the graph shows.

4 Draw a line of best fit onto the scatter diagram.

5 Use the line of best fit to estimate the possible height of a woman weighing:

   a 60 kg   **b** 63 kg

6 Use the line of best fit to estimate the possible weight of a woman who is:

   a 145 cm tall   **b** 168 cm tall

Teacher's tips

When drawing a line of best fit try to have the line as close as possible to all points, with an equal number of points above and below the line. The best fit line does not need to start at (0,0).

49: Probability (1)

You will revise:
▶ how to find probabilities using equally likely outcomes.

Get started

Probability is about the chance, or likelihood, of something happening. The probability of something happening can be measured in several ways:

▶ seeing how often it has happened before
▶ by doing an experiment
▶ using equally likely outcomes.

To find a probability using equally likely outcomes you can use this formula:

$$\text{Probability } (P) = \frac{\text{the number of things you want}}{\text{the number of equally likely outcomes}}$$

Practice

1 Use equally likely outcomes to write the probabilities of these events as fractions.

   a Tossing a coin to land on heads.

   b Rolling a number 3 on a normal dice.

   c Choosing at random a day of the week starting with the letter S.

Challenge

2 Use equally likely outcomes to write the probabilities of these events as fractions.

   a Choosing at random a vowel from the alphabet.

   b Choosing at random an ace from a pack of cards.

   c Choosing at random a diamond from a pack of cards.

   d Rolling an even number on a normal dice.

   e Rolling a multiple of 3 on a normal dice.

   f Rolling a number greater than 6 on a normal dice.

3 One of these cards is picked at random.

| 0 | 1 | 2 | 3 | 4 | 5 | 6 | 7 | 8 | 9 |

What is the probability that it will:

a be a 4?
b not be a 4?

c be a number greater than 5?
d not be a number greater than 5?

e be a square number?
f not be a square number?

g be a prime number?
h not be a prime number?

4 Kate has 8 cards, numbered 1 to 8. She picks one at random. Mark on a 0–1 probability scale the probability that the number is greater than 5.

5 There are 8 teams left in the quarter finals of the cup. The names are written onto cards and put into a bag. They will be picked at random.

| Arsenal | Liverpool | Derby County | Manchester United |

| Leeds United | Leicester City | Southampton | Oxford United |

Write the probability, as a fraction in its simplest form, of the first club drawn from the bag:

a being Arsenal
b beginning with a vowel

c beginning with an 'L'
d ending with a 'd'

e containing a 'p'
f containing an 'e'

g consisting of two words
h having an odd number of letters

i containing 11 letters
j containing 12 letters

k beginning and ending with the same letter

l containing two consecutive letters in the same sequence as they appear in the alphabet, e.g. ab.

6 A spinner is made from a regular dodecagon (12 sides).
The probability of spinning each colour is:

$\frac{1}{4}$ red $\frac{1}{3}$ yellow $\frac{1}{6}$ green $\frac{1}{12}$ blue $\frac{2}{12}$ pink

How many sections are shaded for each colour?

How did I do?

I can find probabilities using equally likely outcomes.

Teacher's tips

Defining the total number of *equally likely* outcomes is key to calculating probability. This total includes the target outcome itself. To compare probabilities, first express them as fractions with common denominators, or convert them to percentages.

You will revise:
▶ experimental and theoretical probability.

Get started

Probability is about the chance, or likelihood, of something happening. Probabilities can be expressed as fractions, decimals or as percentages. The probabilities of **mutually exclusive events** have a total of 1.

To find a theoretical or experimental probability you can use these formulae:

$$\text{Theoretical probability} = \frac{\text{the number of things you want}}{\text{the number of equally likely outcomes}}$$

$$\text{Experimental probability} = \frac{\text{number of times the event has happened}}{\text{total number of results}}$$

Practice

1 Answer these questions.

a What is the theoretical probability that a day of the week picked at random will contain the letter U?

b If the theoretical probability that it will rain today is $\frac{2}{9}$, what is the theoretical probability that it will NOT rain today?

c One playing card was randomly picked from a full pack. This was repeated 100 times. A heart was picked 28 times. What is the experimental probability of picking a heart? Write your answer as a fraction in its simplest form, as a decimal and as a percentage.

Challenge

2 An experiment was conducted where a coloured ball was picked at random from a bag, its colour noted and the ball replaced. Three experiments like this were conducted, each with the ball being replaced a different number of times. The results are shown in these tables.

Experiment 1		
Red	Blue	Green
4	13	3

Experiment 2		
Red	Blue	Green
13	29	8

Experiment 3		
Red	Blue	Green
25	63	12

a Write the experimental probability for each set of results as a fraction in its simplest form, as a decimal and as a percentage.

b Which of these descriptions do you think is most likely to be the set of balls used for all three experiments?

Set A: 10 red balls, 10 blue balls, 5 green balls

Set B: 25 red balls, 50 blue balls, 25 green balls

Set C: 10 red balls, 25 blue balls, 5 green balls

Set D: 30 red balls, 50 blue balls, 20 green balls

3 Each table shows the theoretical probabilities (as decimals) of picking coloured cubes from a bag. Write the number of cubes of each colour in the bags. Present your answer as a table.

Bag K: 90 cubes		
Red	Blue	Green
0.1	0.7	0.2

Bag L: 70 cubes		
Red	Blue	Green
0.5	0.2	0.3

Bag M: 40 cubes		
Red	Blue	Green
0.05	0.65	0.3

Bag N: 60 cubes		
Red	Blue	Green
0.45	0.15	0.4

4 **a** Add the experiment probabilities from the three experiments in question 2 together with the results of this experiment.

Experiment 4		
Red	Blue	Green
4	13	3

b Using your results, predict the number of red, blue and green balls there were in the bag if the total number of balls was 80.

5 Comment on this statement. Do you agree?

When playing the lottery I would not choose the numbers that won last week's jackpot as they are less likely to come up next week.

How did I do?

I can estimate probabilities based on experimental data. ☐

I can use relative frequency as an estimate of probability. ☐

Teacher's tips

Experimental probability can be different from theoretical probability; it is based upon results from a set of trials. If a coin thrown 60 times lands on heads 27 times the experimental probability of a head is 9/20 (vs. ½ theoretical probability).

Answers

1: Place value and standard form

1
- **a** 34 000
- **b** 6 500 000
- **c** 2200
- **d** 375 000 000
- **e** 270 000
- **f** 1.1
- **g** 29.7
- **h** 0.654

2
- **a** 350 000
- **b** 94 000
- **c** 6800
- **d** 0.0743
- **e** 0.42
- **f** 0.001 95

3
- **a** 470 000
- **b** 432
- **c** 9 780 000
- **d** 55 000
- **e** 48
- **f** 7
- **g** 0.12
- **h** 0.086
- **i** 0.007

4 A, D, F, I

5
- **a** 3.4×10^7
- **b** 2.3×10^5
- **c** 7.87×10^3
- **d** 5×10^4
- **e** 1.25×10^7
- **f** 2.34×10^7
- **g** 4×10^{-3}
- **h** 2×10^{-6}
- **i** 6.5×10^{-5}
- **j** 3.28×10^{-3}

6
- **a** 4.8×10^4, 48×10^3, $4.8 \times 10\,000$
- **b** 125×10^3, 1.25×10^5
- **c** 4.2×10^{-3}, 4.2×0.001, 42×10^{-4}

7
- **a** 4.8×10^4
- **b** 1.25×10^5
- **c** 4.2×10^{-3}

Try it yourself!
The smallest is 1.2×10^{-5}; the largest is 4.5×10^7.

2: Fractions

1
- **a** $\frac{2}{5}$
- **b** $\frac{11}{12}$
- **c** $\frac{13}{21}$
- **d** $\frac{13}{20}$
- **e** $\frac{17}{24}$
- **f** $\frac{1}{2}$
- **g** $\frac{3}{20}$
- **h** $\frac{11}{40}$

2
- **a** $\frac{14}{15}$
- **b** $\frac{13}{24}$
- **c** $1\frac{9}{56}$ or $\frac{65}{56}$
- **d** $1\frac{29}{30}$ or $\frac{59}{30}$
- **e** $\frac{13}{18}$
- **f** $\frac{43}{70}$
- **g** $\frac{7}{24}$
- **h** $\frac{23}{42}$

3
- **a** $\frac{10}{21}$
- **b** $\frac{2}{3}$
- **c** $\frac{16}{45}$
- **d** $\frac{3}{14}$
- **e** $\frac{5}{48}$
- **f** $\frac{5}{42}$

4
- **a** $2\frac{5}{8}$ or $\frac{21}{8}$
- **b** $\frac{10}{27}$
- **c** $\frac{6}{7}$
- **d** $7\frac{7}{8}$ or $\frac{63}{8}$
- **e** $1\frac{3}{5}$ or $\frac{8}{5}$
- **f** $1\frac{1}{6}$ or $\frac{7}{6}$
- **g** $1\frac{1}{7}$ or $\frac{8}{7}$
- **h** $\frac{40}{63}$

5
- **a** $\frac{9}{10}$
- **b** $\frac{3}{20}$
- **c** $\frac{1}{3}$
- **d** $\frac{2}{33}$
- **e** $\frac{1}{3}$
- **f** $\frac{2}{7}$
- **g** $\frac{1}{6}$
- **h** $\frac{3}{20}$

6
- **a** $\frac{9}{16}$
- **b** $\frac{1}{9}$
- **c** $\frac{7}{15}$
- **d** $1\frac{1}{4}$ or $\frac{5}{4}$
- **e** $1\frac{1}{2}$ or $\frac{3}{2}$
- **f** $1\frac{13}{14}$ or $\frac{27}{14}$
- **g** $1\frac{3}{4}$ or $\frac{7}{4}$
- **h** $\frac{1}{3}$

Try it yourself!
$\frac{7}{10} \div \frac{14}{20}$

3: Percentages (1)

1 a 120, 60, 24, 2.4

   b 80, 40, 16, 1.6

2 a £14   b 18 m

   c £22   d 150 g

   e 53 cm   f 2.5 m

3 a 180, 72, 12, 4.8   b 48, 3.2, 24, 96

4 a £36   b 6 m

   c £4   d 10 kg

   e 54 cm   f 66 m

   g 63 mm   h 18 cm

   i 19 cm

5 a £21   b £1200

   c 99 ounces

6 a 180, 90, 36, 18, 3.6, 1.8

   b 216, 270, 54, 91.8, 39.6, 21.6,
      183.6, 126, 181.8, 57.6, 237.6, 55.8

7 a £397.10   b £794.20

   c £1588.40

8 a 2% of 250, 4% of 250, 6% of 250

   b For £250, even-numbered percentages are whole numbers of pounds.

4: Percentages (2)

1 a £18.80   b £7.26

   c £33.06   d 11.57 kg

   e 6.65 kg   f 21.60 kg

   g 4.77 ml   h 3.75 m

   i 13.77 ml

2 £302 600

3 79.68 kg

4 a 96.48 m   b £191 250

   c 30.68 km   d 592.2 g

   e £11 055   f 41.678 kg

   g 1746 ml   h 75.442 cm

   i 49.536 mm   j £86.02

   k 5.5734 kg   l 171.19 m

5

Amount to be increased or decreased by	New price	New price as percentage of original price
£9.01	£62.01	100% + 17% = 117%
£76	£874	100% − 8% = 92%
£166.95	£431.95	100% + 63% = 163%
£432	£768	100% − 36% = 64%
£36 450	£81 450	100% + 81% = 181%
£84 100	£205 900	100% − 29% = 71%

6 a £58   b £37

   c £28   d 40 mph

   e 78.6 kg

5: Direct proportion

1   a 56, 700   b 56, 160

    c 8.25, 11.25

2   a £11.22   b £2.61

    c £5.85   d £34.60

    e £2.91   f £4.11

3   a $c = 2.25n$ b $c = 3.5n$

    c $c = 1.75n$

4   All statements show direct proportionality.

5   a $C = \pi d$ b $P = 6l$

    c $A = \pi r^2$ d $A = l^2$

6   Bar B

6: Ratio

1   a £1.02, £1.36   b £16.72, £2.09

    c £3.81, £11.43, £15.24

2   a 7 : 4   b 1 : 6

    c 15 : 1   d 1 : 26

    e 5 : 4   f 3 : 16

    g 8 : 1 : 2   h 6 : 10 : 15

3   a 1 : 4.5   b 1 : 1.8

    c 1 : 2.13   d 1 : 1.57

    e 1 : 1.67   f 1 : 1.56

    g 1 : 0.81   h 1 : 52.5

4   6.65 g copper, 2.3275 g zinc, 0.5225 g nickel

5   a

Player	aces : double faults	games won : games lost
Sandy	1 : 0.8	1 : 0.58
Roger	1 : 0.5	1 : 0.19
Maria	1 : 8	1 : 1.58
Vera	1 : 2	1 : 0.49
Justine	1 : 3.5	1 : 1.2

    b Roger Fedwell

    c Roger Fedwell

6   T-shirt A, P : C = 1 : 2.5
    T-shirt B, P : C = 1 : 1.4
    T-shirt C, P : C = 1 : 0.57
    T-shirt D, P : C = 1 : 1.55
    T-shirt A has the highest ratio of cotton.

7: Positive and negative numbers

1   a 3   b −5

    c 4   d 5

    e 4

2   a −5   b −3

    c −12   d −7

    e −9

3   a 4, −14, −4   b −9, 5, −5

    c −4, −26, 4

4   a −12   b −11

    c 7   d −14

    e 4   f −25

    g −7   h −32

    i −17   j −45

5   a −6 + 4 = −2

    b −5 − 8 = −13

    c 5 − 9 = −4

    d 3 + 5 = 8

    e −9 − 3 = −12

    f 15 + 11 = 26

    g 17 − 5 = 12

    h −18 − 4 = −22

6   a −2   b −4

    c −2   d −5

7   a −6 + 4   b 8 + −6

    c −11 − −9   d −9 − −11

8 a

0	−1	4
5	1	−3
−2	3	2

b

−2	−3	2
3	−1	−5
−4	1	0

Try it yourself!

−4	−5	0
1	−3	−7
−6	−1	−2

8: Integers

1 a 30   b −30

   c −7   d 5

   e −80   f 24

   g 6   h −8

2 a 56   b −90

   c −8   d 6

   e −40   f 54

   g 8   h −9

   i 36   j −48

   k 9   l −8

3 a 25   b 9

   c 49   d 100

   e 81   f 16

   g 64   h 36

4 a ±4   b ±2

   c ±9   d ±8

   e ±11   f ±7

   g ±6   h ±12

5 a 24, −24, −24, 24, −56, 56, −56, 56

   b 8, 8, −8, −8, 7, −7, −7, 7

   c 8100, 144, 3600, 121, 4900, 6400, 900, 2500

6 Multiplications can be in any order.

   a −6 × 4, −8 × 3, 12 × −2

   b −6 × −8, 4 × 12

   c −4 × 12, −6 × 8

   d −2 × 12 × 4, −4 × 3 × 8, −6 × −2 × −8, 3 × 4 × −8

9: Prime numbers, factors and multiples

1

×	1	2	3	4	5	6	7	8	9	10	11	12
3	3	6	9	12	15	18	21	24	27	30	33	36
4	4	8	12	16	20	24	28	32	36	40	44	48
5	5	10	15	20	25	30	35	40	45	50	55	60
6	6	12	18	24	30	36	42	48	54	60	66	72
7	7	14	21	28	35	42	49	56	63	70	77	84
8	8	16	24	32	40	48	56	64	72	80	88	96
9	9	18	27	36	45	54	63	72	81	90	99	108

2 a 12   b 21

   c 56   d 18

   e 40   f 18

   g 36   h 60

3 a 1, 2, 4, 5, 10, 20

   b 1, 2, 4, 8, 16

   c 1, 5, 25,

   d 1, 2, 3, 5, 6, 10, 15, 30

   e 1, 2, 7, 14,

   f 1, 3, 9, 27

   g 1, 17

   h 1, 5, 7, 35

   i 1, 2, 3, 4, 6, 9, 12, 18, 36

   j 1, 2, 4, 8, 16, 32

4 17

5 12, 18, 20, 28

6 a 7   b 4

   c 1   d 10

   e 16   f 5

   g 6   h 2

   i 3

7 4, 9, 16, 25. They are square numbers.

8 a 7 + 2   b 11 + 5 or 13 + 3

   c 23 + 2   d 31 + 5 or 29 + 7

   e 47 + 2   f 61 + 3 or 59 + 5

   g 79 + 2   h 97 + 3

9 a 1   b 96

   c 96

10: Prime numbers

1 a $30 = 2 \times 3 \times 5$ b $28 = 2^2 \times 7$

   c $90 = 2 \times 3^2 \times 5$ d $150 = 2 \times 3 \times 5^2$

2 a $16 = 2^4$ b $144 = 2^4 \times 3^2$

   c $200 = 2^3 \times 5^2$ d $135 = 3^3 \times 5$

   e $180 = 2^2 \times 3^2 \times 5$ f $63 = 3^2 \times 7$

   g $120 = 2^3 \times 3 \times 5$ h $76 = 2^2 \times 19$

   i $512 = 2^9$ j $343 = 7^3$

   k $125 = 5^3$ l $175 = 5^2 \times 7$

3 a $2^3 = 8$ b $2^6 \times 7 = 448$

4 a $2^3 \times 3^2 = 72$ b $2^4 \times 3^3 = 432$

5 a $2 \times 3^2 = 18$

   b $2^2 \times 3^3 \times 5^2 \times 7 = 18\,900$

6 a $2^2 = 4$

   b $2^4 \times 3 \times 7 = 336$

7 a $2^2 = 4$

   b $2^3 \times 3 \times 7 \times 11 = 1848$

Try it yourself!

a 2, 4, 8, 16, 32, 64, 128

b 3, 9, 27, 81

c 5, 25, 125

1 **a** 25 **b** 36

   c 9 **d** 49

   e 100 **f** 4

   g 64 **h** 81

   i 144 **j** 121

2 **a** 8 **b** 1

   c 27 **d** 64

   e 1000

3 **a** 25 **b** ± 7

   c ± 9 **d** 36

   e 100 **f** 121

   g ± 4 **h** 64

   i ± 10 **j** 144

4 **a** 225 **b** ± 17

   c 1024 **d** ± 22

   e 361 **f** 512

   g 6 **h** 9

   i 1331 **j** 1728

5 **a** correct **b** correct

   c correct **d** incorrect; $\sqrt[3]{125} = 5$

   e incorrect; $(0.01)^2 = 0.0001$

   f incorrect; $\sqrt[3]{3375} = 15$

   g incorrect; $\sqrt[3]{35.937} = 3.3$

   h correct

6 **a** 144 **b** 216

   c 30.25 **d** 512

   e ± 64 **f** 21

   g 196 **h** 162

   i ± 5 **j** ± 10

   k 0 **l** 512

   m 144 **n** 25

   o 400 **p** 13

   q ± 13 **r** 196

   s ± 162 **t** 216

7 **a** $27^2 = 729$

   b $31^2 = 961$

   c $49^2 = 2401$ or $59^2 = 3481$

   d $77^2 = 5929$

   e $6^3 = 216$ or $8^3 = 512$

   f $21^3 = 9261$

   g $15^3 = 3375$

   h $25^3 = 15\,625$ or $33^3 = 35\,937$ or $44^3 = 85\,184$

   i $(25 + 44)^3 = 328\,509$

1 a $5 \times 5 \times 5$

   b $6 \times 6 \times 6 \times 6 \times 6 \times 6$

   c $3 \times 3 \times 3 \times 3 \times 3$

   d $7 \times 7 \times 7 \times 7$

   e $10 \times 10 \times 10$

   f $2 \times 2 \times 2 \times 2 \times 2 \times 2 \times 2$

   g $n \times n \times n \times n$

   h $a \times a \times a \times a \times a$

   i $p \times p \times p \times p \times p \times p \times p \times p$

2 a 6^5 b 2^7

   c 5^7 d 10^{14}

   e 8^8 f 6^5

   g 3^{10} h 4^{16}

   i n^5 j a^{12}

   k x^5 l y^{11}

   m f^{10} n g^4

   o d^5 p m^6

3 a 7^5 b 4^6

   c 2^4 d 8^3

   e 6^2 f 9^1

   g a^4 h y^4

   i p^2 j s^4

   k m^1 l w^2

   m 5^2 n 9^5

   o 7^3 p a^6

   q m^3 r y^2

4 a $3^{-2} = \dfrac{1}{3^2}$ b $2^{-6} = \dfrac{1}{2^6}$

   c $8^{-4} = \dfrac{1}{8^4}$ d $m^{-7} = \dfrac{1}{m^7}$

   e $p^{-5} = \dfrac{1}{p^5}$ f $k^{-4} = \dfrac{1}{k^4}$

5 a $\frac{1}{4}$ b 16

   c $\frac{1}{16}$ d $\frac{1}{3}$

   e $\frac{1}{25}$ f $\frac{1}{36}$

   g $\frac{1}{1000}$ h $\frac{1}{7}$

   i 16   j $\frac{1}{16}$

   k $\frac{1}{32}$ l $\frac{1}{15}$

Try it yourself!

$\frac{1}{5} = 5^{-1}$

1 a 0   b 1

   c 0   d 1

   e 0   f 0

   g 58   h 0

   i 1   j 0

   k 1   l 0

2 a false   b true

   c true   d false

   e true   f true

3 a 33   b 30

   c 8   d 12

   e 13   f 2

   g 10   h 36

   i 15   j 13

   k 10   l 3

   m 36   n 30

   o 19

4 A, B, E, F

5 a $264 + 264 + 264$ b $7530 + 753$

   c $1034 \div 22$ d $9320 - 932$

   e $2448 \div 72$ f $3600 + 36$

   g 3670   h $87\,400 - 874$

6 a true   b true

   c true   d false

   e true   f false

Try it yourself!

a $8 \times 4 + 2$ b $8 + 4 \times 2$

c $(8 + 2) \times 4$ d $(4 + 2) \times 8$

14: Calculations

1
a	51	b	32
c	12	d	17
e	13	f	9
g	50	h	100
i	24	j	21
k	20	l	5
m	55	n	40
o	22		

2
a	3	b	4
c	15	d	3
e	10	f	2
g	3	h	2

3
a	25	b	49
c	6.4	d	4

4   Examples include

$4 \times (2 + 3) - 2^2 \times 7 + 1 = -7$

$4 \times 2 + 3 - (2^2 \times 7) + 1 = -16$

$4 \times 2 + (3 - 2^2) \times 7 + 1 = 2$

$4 \times (2 + 3) - 2^2 \times (7 + 1) = -12$

$4 \times 2 + (3 - 2)^2 \times 7 + 1 = 16$

$4 \times 2 + (3 - 2^2) \times (7 + 1) = 0$

$4 \times 2 + 3 - 2^2 \times (7 + 1) = -21$

$4 \times 2 + (3 - 2)^2 \times (7 + 1) = 16$

$4 \times 2 + 3 - (2^2 \times 7 + 1) = -18$

$(4 \times 2 + 3 - 2)^2 \times 7 + 1 = 568$

$(4 \times 2 + 3 - 2)^2 \times (7 + 1) = 648$

$4 \times (2 + 3 - 2)^2 \times 7 + 1 = 253$

$4 \times (2 + 3 - 2)^2 \times (7 + 1) = 288$

$(4 \times 2) + 3 - 2^2 \times 7 + 1 = -16$

5
a	12	b	12
c	28	d	18

6
a	500	b	2.60
c	88.93	d	18.96
e	125.48	f	9.80
g	42.88	h	80.02
i	7.06	j	1.78

Try it yourself!

−108

$50 \div (25 - 15) \times (7 - 5) = 10$

15: Calculations and rounding

1

Number	To whole number	1 d.p.	2 d.p.	3 d.p.
32.1502	32	32.2	32.15	32.150
86.8309	87	86.8	86.83	86.831
69.6065	70	69.6	69.61	69.607
19.989	20	20.0	19.99	19.989
6.4993	6	6.5	6.50	6.499
0.0893	0	0.1	0.09	0.089

2
a	700 000	b	2000
c	9000	d	60 000
e	5	f	20
g	5000	h	200
i	3000	j	900
k	5	l	20
m	4	n	20
o	30	p	700

3
a	0.007	b	0.03
c	0.9	d	0.000 06
e	0.06	f	0.5
g	0.8	h	0.002
i	0.06	j	0.000 001
k	0.05	l	0.01

4 **a** $6000 \times 50 = 300\,000$

    b $400 \div 8 = 50$

    c $6 \times 3 = 18$

    d $8 \times 6 = 48$

    e $(8000 \div 2000) \times 2000 = 8000$

    f $\sqrt{36} \times 20 = 120$

    g $(0.01 \times 200)^2 = 4$

5 **a** $(0.008 \div 2) \times 7 = 0.028$

    b $(0.6 \div 3) \times 2 = 0.4$

    c $0.08 \times 0.02 \times 0.4 = 0.000\,64$

    d $(6 \times 4) \div 0.5 = 48$

    e $(0.04 \times 0.05) \div (0.1)^2 = 0.002 \div 0.01 = 0.2$

    f $(0.03 \times 20)^2 = (0.6)^2 = 0.36$

    g $(0.004 \times 2000)^2 \div 0.8 = 64 \div 0.8 = 80$

Try it yourself!
40.6

16: Problem solving (1)

1 **a** division   **b** multiplication

    c division   **d** addition

    e subtraction

2 **a** 144   **b** 6839

    c 6   **d** 68

    e 728   **f** 15p

    g 34   **h** £5

    i 27   **j** 14

    k 19   **l** 44p

    m 20p   **n** £1.20

    o 8 boxes; 7 full   **p** 15

    q 12   **r** £13

    s 25% of £5   **t** £173 964

    u £114.75

Try it yourself!
The footballer earns more.
The footballer earns £438 000 in a year.
The supermodel earns £404 712 in a year.

17: Using a calculator

1 **a** $\frac{2}{5}$ **b** $\frac{47}{100}$

    c $\frac{4}{9}$ **d** $\frac{9}{14}$

    e $\frac{1}{4}$ **f** $\frac{1}{16}$

    g $5\frac{11}{16}$ **h** $8\frac{9}{10}$

    i $9\frac{4}{9}$ **j** $5\frac{3}{7}$

    k $3\frac{2}{7}$ **l** $2\frac{3}{4}$

2 **a** 0.875   **b** 1.25

    c 0.1111 . . .   **d** 0.3333 . . .

    e 0.7777 . . .   **f** 1.1111 . . .

    g 0.9375   **h** 2.375

    i 1.2222 . . .   **j** 5.4444 . . .

    k 5.875   **l** 6.8888 . . .

3 **a** 0.2222 . . .   **b** 0.4444 . . .

    c 1.75   **d** 0.6666 . . .

    e 2.5555. . . .   **f** 6.1111. . . .

    g 1.2222 . . .   **h** 0.375

    i 1.375

4 **a** $\frac{1}{16}$ **b** $9\frac{3}{40}$

    c $3\frac{71}{250}$ **d** $\frac{11}{80}$

    e $5\frac{3}{500}$ **f** $\frac{289}{400}$

    g $8\frac{1}{8}$ **h** $\frac{13}{16}$

    i $6\frac{111}{125}$ **j** $9\frac{31}{200}$

    k $\frac{31}{40}$ **l** $4\frac{221}{500}$

5 **a** 0.27272727 . . . , 0.36363636 . . . ,
0.45454545 . . . , 0.54545454 . . . ,
0.63636363 . . . , 0.72727272 . . . ,
0.81818181 . . . , 0.90909090 . . .

    b 0.03030303 . . . , 0.04040404 . . . ,
0.05050505 . . . , 0.06060606 . . . ,
0.07070707 . . . , 0.08080808 . . . ,
0.09090909 . . . , 0.10101010 . . .

6 **a** $\frac{10}{99}$ **b** $\frac{20}{99}$

    c $\frac{8}{99}$ **d** $4\frac{1}{2}$

    e $40\frac{1}{2}$ **f** $\frac{5}{99}$

18: Problem solving (2)

1 **a** 11p **b** 141

   c £22 **d** 28

   e 31 **f** 70p

2 **a** 426 **b** 280

   c 8 **d** 29

   e 14

3 **a** 6 years **b** cheaper, by £26

   c 75% of £80 **d** 25% of £2.60

   e £317 148

4 **a** 20 and 64 **b** 28 and 18

   c There are 3 fish and 7 people.

   d There are 6 cows and 6 people.

   e There are 4 cats and 4 people.

   f There are 3 fish, 5 dogs and 4 people.

Try it yourself!
61

19: Trial and improvement

1 **a** *a* must lie between 8 and 9.

   b *b* must lie between 5 and 6.

   c *c* must lie between 9 and 10.

   d *x* must lie between 3 and 4.

2 *x* = 3.74

3 **a** *a* must lie between 3 and 4.

   b *b* must lie between 2 and 3.

   c *c* must lie between 1 and 2.

   d *x* must lie between 3 and 4.

4 *x* = 3.78

5 *x* = 4.75

6 *x* = 6.29

Try it yourself!

4

20: Simplifying expressions (1)

1 **a** $x + 6y$ **b** $m + 3n$

   c $5s + t$ **d** $6e + 2f$

   e $5j + 2k$ **f** $6c - 3d$

   g $v + w$

2 **a** $5m - 5n + 7$ **b** $2s + 3t + 7$

   c $5g - h + 6$ **d** $3x + 4y - 3$

   e $c - 3$ **f** $6s + t - 3$

   g $e + 6f + 3$ **h** $-8j + k$

3 **a** $m + 1$ **b** $3s + 1$

   c $19g + 17$

4 **a** $15a - 10$ **b** $12m + 18$

   c $7p + 35$ **d** $24y - 32$

   e $20 - 10n$ **f** $28 - 24f$

5 **a** $7a + 10$ **b** $-3m + 33$

   c $23p + 11$ **d** $7y + 14$

6 **a** b^4 **b** a^5

   c $3g$ **d** $4m$

   e n^6 **f** $5s$

   g $3t$ **h** w^4

   i e^7 **j** y^6

   k $8v$ **l** p^3

   m $7f$ **n** j^{10}

   o k^5

7 **a** $3a + 26$ **b** $-9m + 1$

   c $-15p + 21$ **d** $3y$

   e $8q + 4$

Try it yourself!
Any four expressions equivalent to $8x - 2y - 4$

1 **a** $12a - 8$ **b** $18m + 27$

c $2p + 10$ **d** $15y - 20$

e $16 - 8n$ **f** $42 - 36f$

g $70 - 20m$ **h** $24 - 6b$

2 **a** $21p + 39$ **b** $9e + 9$

c $15m + 34$ **d** $20n + 29$

e $16a - 22$ **f** $21y - 8$

g $23y + 5$ **h** $9g + 42$

3 **a** $-2p + 37$ **b** $6e - 13$

c $8m - 18$ **d** $9n + 9$

4 **a** $8ab - 16bc$ **b** $12kp + 18k$

c $2p^2 + 10pq$ **d** $30y^2 - 10y$

e $16n - 8n^2$ **f** $-3x^2y - 9xy^2$

g $-14ef + 6e^2$ **h** $-25x^2 + 5x$

5 **a** $4(p + 2)$ **b** $3(2d + e)$

c $3(3m + 2n)$ **d** $2(x + 6y)$

e $10(3p + q)$ **f** $3(6a - 7b)$

g $4(4p - 5r)$ **h** $2(5s - 4t)$

6 **a** $n(n - 1)$ **b** $a(3 + 5b)$

c $5e(d + 3)$ **d** $3c(3 + 2c)$

e $2y(x + 4)$ **f** $10c(ab + d)$

g $4m(1 - 3m)$ **h** $5x(x - 3)$

i $5t(2s + 1)$ **j** $5p(3q - 1)$

k $6(t - 1)$ **l** $2g(4 - 9g)$

Try it yourself!
Example answers:
$2x(4x - 8y)$, $8(x^2 - 2xy)$, $8x^2 - 16xy$, $x(8x - 16y)$ etc.

1 **a** 14

b cheaper by £1

c 75% of 45 km

d 36% of 40 kg

e £297 648

2 **a** No, they are 26 and 17.

b 36 and 16

c 169 and 36

d 50

3 **a** $\frac{67}{80}$ **b** 1056

c £3.50   **d** $\frac{1}{7}$

e There are 7 fish, 6 dogs, and 3 people.

f 58.333 cm

4 **a** No

b Yes, possible answers are 12, 24, 36, 48.

c 9 m

d Yes

Try it yourself!
180

23: Equations

1 **a** $a = 9$ **b** $y = 5.875$

 c $f = 9.4$ **d** $y = 4.25$

 e $n = 6.625$ **f** $g = 4.2$

2 **a** $h = 5$ **b** $k = 9$

 c $c = 12$ **d** $g = -0.8$

 e $x = 7.25$ **f** $p = 30.5$

 g $h = 13.5$ **h** $j = 5.25$

 i $k = 3.1$ **j** $m = 8.333$ (3 d.p.) or $8\frac{1}{3}$

 k $f = 2$ **l** $p = 6.388$ (3 d.p.) or $6\frac{7}{18}$

3 **a** $f = 2$ **b** $b = 5$

 c $d = 2.5$ **d** $a = 5$

 e $e = 2.5$ **f** $c = 5$

 g $g = 7$ **h** $h = 3.5$

 i $j = 2.333$ (3 d.p.) or $2\frac{1}{3}$

 j $m = -1.333$ (3 d.p.) or $-1\frac{1}{3}$

 k $p = 2.1$

 l $s = 3$

4 **a** $r = 9.6$

 b $t = -1.333$ (3 d.p.) or $-1\frac{1}{3}$

 c $u = 12$

 d $m = -1.666$ (3 d.p.) or $-1\frac{2}{3}$

 e $k = -45$

 f $n = 10\frac{1}{9}$

5 **a** $m = 16.5$, length $= 200$

 b $s = 5\frac{5}{12}$, length $= 101.25$

 c $n = -0.875$, length $= 13.5$

Try it yourself!
-8.25

24: Formulae and substituting (1)

1 **a** £6 **b** £8

 c £16 **d** £22

 e £18 **f** £30

2 **a** £14 **b** £17

 c £26 **d** £23

 e £20 **f** £35

 g £29 **h** £41

3 **a** 19 **b** 25

 c 61

4 **a** 28 **b** 34

 c 54 **d** 0

5 **a** $P \approx 14$ **b** $P \approx 21$

 c $P \approx 42$ **d** $P \approx 49$

 e $P \approx 56$ **f** $P \approx 77$

 g $P \approx 140$ **h** $P \approx 175$

 i $P \approx 84$

6 **a** 19 **b** 18

 c 24 **d** 26

 e 35

7 **a** F, $W = 3(7 - n)$

 b G, $W = 2(n + 4)$

 c C, $W = 5n - 3$

 d E, $W = n^2$

8 $P = 3N + 1$

25: Formulae and substituting (2)

1. a 84 b −7
    c 27 d 40
    e 22 f 153
    g 46 h 20
    i 14.5

2. a 176.63 cm² b 91.13 cm³
    c 13 cm d 75.2 cm²

3. a $D = ST$ b $a = \dfrac{F}{m}$
    c $r = \sqrt{\dfrac{A}{\pi}}$ d $a = \dfrac{v - u}{t}$
    e $l = \sqrt[3]{V}$

4. $C = \dfrac{5(F - 32)}{9}$

5. $r = \sqrt[3]{\dfrac{3V}{4\pi}}$

6. $l = g\left(\dfrac{T}{2\pi}\right)^2$

Try it yourself!

$u = \dfrac{fv}{v - f}$

26: Sequences (1)

1. a 9, 14, 19, 24, 29
    b 0, 3, 6, 9, 12
    c 14, 12, 10, 8, 6

2. a 5, 10, 15, 20, 25
    b 7, 12, 17, 22, 27
    c 4, 9, 14, 19, 24

3. a nth term = $6n$; 10th term = 60
    b nth term = $2n$; 10th term = 20
    c nth term = $8n$; 10th term = 80
    d nth term = $5n + 1$; 10th term = 51

4. a 3, 6, 9, 12
    b $3n$
    c 30

5. a 4, 7, 10, 13
    b $3n + 1$
    c 31

6. $4n + 1$

7. Any sequences that meet the criteria such as:

    a 3, 6, 9, 12, 15, 18, . . .

    First term is 3; each term increases by 3.

    Multiply the position number by 3.

    b 1, 3, 5, 7, 9, 11, 13, . . .

    First term is 1; each term increases by 2.

    Multiply the position number by 2 and subtract 1.

    c 7, 17, 27, 37, 47, . . .

    First term is 7; each term increases by 10.

    Multiply the position number by 10 and subtract 3.

27: Sequences (2)

1 **a** 7, 14, 21, 28, 35

   b 9, 16, 23, 30, 37

   c 6, 13, 20, 27, 34

2 **a** $6n - 2$ **b** $5n - 3$

   c $2n + 10$ **d** $7n - 4$

   e $4n - 13$ **f** $2n - 1$

3 **a** 598   **b** 497

   c 210   **d** 696

   e 387   **f** 199

4 **a** $n^2 + 1$ **b** $2n^2$

   c $n^2 - 2$ **d** $5n^2$

5 **a** 101   **b** 200

   c 98   **d** 500

Try it yourself!
The rule for the nth term is $4n + 2$ if it is a linear sequence with a constant difference between terms.

28: Functions

1 **a**

1	2	3	4	5	6
0	3	6	9	12	15

Check that the mapping diagram shows the above values for $x = 1$ to $x = 6$.

   b

1	2	3	4	5	6
0	2	4	6	8	10

Check that the mapping diagram shows the above values for $x = 1$ to $x = 6$.

2 **a** The two-tier mapping diagram should show
   $1 \to 1 \to 1$, $2 \to 3 \to 2$, $3 \to 5 \to 3$, $4 \to 7 \to 4$,
   $5 \to 9 \to 5$.

   b The functions are inverses of each other.

3 **a** The two-tier mapping diagram should show
   $1 \to 8 \to 1$, $2 \to 7 \to 2$, $3 \to 6 \to 3$, $4 \to 5 \to 4$,
   $5 \to 4 \to 5$, $6 \to 3 \to 6$, $7 \to 2 \to 7$, $8 \to 1 \to 8$.

   b The functions are inverses of each other.

   c Yes.

4 **a** $x \to (x - 1)/2$ **b** $x \to (x + 2)/3$

   c $x \to 2(x + 5)$ **d** $x \to x/6 - 4$

   e $x \to (x - 4)/8$ **f** $x \to (x + 3)/7$

   g $x \to 4(x - 1)$ **h** $x \to x/3 - 1$

   i $x \to (5 - x)/2$ **j** $x \to 4(x - 5)$

   k $x \to 3x - 4$ **l** $x \to 5x + 3$

5 Check of answers to question 4 using two-tiered mapping diagrams or choosing different values of x to input.

Try it yourself!
Self-inverses are in the form $x \to n - x$, where n is a number.

1 a diagonal   b diagonal

   c vertical   d vertical

   e diagonal   f diagonal

   g horizontal   h diagonal

   i vertical   j diagonal

2 a −1, 1, 3, 5, 7

   b The line should go through (−5, −7) and (2, 7).

3 a 7, 4, 1, −2, −5

   b The line should go through (−2, 7) and (3, −8).

4 approximate coordinates (−0.4, 2.2)

5 a gradient = 2, y intercept = 1

   b gradient = −2, y intercept = −4

   c gradient = 5, y intercept = 0

   d gradient = 1, y intercept = −3

Try it yourself!
$y = -x$ or $x = -y$

1 a

−4	−3	−2	−1	0	1	2	3	4
−19	−15	−11	−7	−3	1	5	9	13

   b See the answer to question 4b below.

   c 4

   d (0, −3)

2 a −3, 5   b 2, −4

   c −1, 0   d 1, 6

   e −1, 5   f 2, −3

3 a $y = 2x - 4$, $y = 2x - 3$

   b $y = -x$, $y = 5 - x$

   c $y = -3x + 5$, $y = 5 - x$

4 a $y = x^2$ values: 16, 9, 4, 1, 0, 1, 4, 9, 16

   b

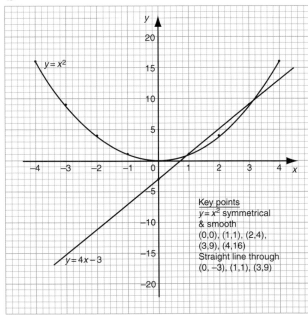

5 (3, 9), (1, 1)

6 a $y = x^2 + 4$ values: 20, 13, 8, 5, 4, 5, 8, 13, 20

   b The curve $y = x^2$ has been translated up 4 places to make $y = x^2 + 4$.

Try it yourself!
$-\frac{1}{4}$

118

31: Problem solving (2)

1 **a** CD = 3x　　　　**b** EF = 3x + 1

　　c 15 cm　　　　　　**d** 22 cm

2 **a** x = 3d　　　　　**b** P = 9d

　　c x = 12 cm　　　　**d** P = 36 cm

　　e d = 10 cm

3 **a** AC = 2r　　　　　**b** AB = d + r

　　c P = 4(d + r)　　　**d** Area = (d + r)^2

4 **a** 20 cm　　　　　　**b** 14.1 cm

　　c 56.4 cm　　　　　**d** 198.81 cm^2

5 Length = 16 cm, width = 8 cm

32: Measurement (1)

1 **a** 300　　　　　　**b** 3

　　c 6　　　　　　　**d** 47

　　e 9　　　　　　　**f** 20

　　g 500　　　　　　**h** 7000

　　i 600　　　　　　**j** 4000

　　k 8　　　　　　　**l** 70 000

2 **a** 1　　　　　　　**b** 7

　　c 4.5　　　　　　**d** 8000

　　e 3500　　　　　　**f** 5700

　　g 1500　　　　　　**h** 2.5

　　i 16 800

3 **a** 370　　　　　　**b** 1.28

　　c 6.7　　　　　　**d** 47.3

　　e 0.986　　　　　**f** 2.38

　　g 4.902　　　　　**h** 0.354

　　i 78

4 **a** 1.2　　　　　　**b** 1.64

　　c 4.362　　　　　**d** 0.866

　　e 3500　　　　　　**f** 5330

　　g 1584　　　　　　**h** 1.647

　　i 16 670

5 **a** 0.15　　　　　　**b** 1

　　c 0.025　　　　　**d** 0.362

　　e 0.013 87　　　　**f** 560

　　g 1.56　　　　　　**h** 0.089

　　i 5.66　　　　　　**j** 8.092

　　k 0.008 67　　　　**l** 81 900

6 **a** false　　　　　**b** true

　　c false　　　　　**d** true

　　e true　　　　　　**f** false

　　g true　　　　　　**h** false

7 Equivalent facts such as: 0.64 m = 640 mm, 0.000 46 km = 46 cm

33: Measurement (2)

1
- a 540
- b 1.62
- c 5.8
- d 26.7
- e 1.7
- f 1.85
- g 7.202
- h 0.877
- i 51
- j 1.7
- k 1.96
- l 4.082
- m 0.834
- n 9500
- o 5210
- p 1876
- q 1.218
- r 24 670

2
- a 30.48
- b 273
- c 8
- d 15.24
- e 318 500
- f 3200

3
- a 4.8
- b 93
- c 9.9
- d 182.28
- e 6.6
- f 66
- g 69.3
- h 2.38

4
- a 8.34
- b 0.095
- c 0.0521
- d 18 760
- e 121 800
- f 246 700

5
- a 4.2
- b 112
- c 1362
- d 8.626
- e 39.6
- f 31.75
- g 3.36
- h 0.096
- i 4544
- j 7.875
- k 40.95
- l 5.28
- m 0.288
- n 2540
- o 3.7488
- p 14.875
- q 910
- r 0.99

34: Constructing triangles

1
- a 7 cm
- b 32°
- c 4.5 cm

2 4.5 cm

3 1.7 cm

4
- a 32°
- b 3.3 cm
- c 120°

5
- a 69°
- b 6.9 cm
- c 5.2 cm

6
- a 58°
- b 7.7 cm
- c 3.2 cm

7 Triangle 1: right-angled scalene
Triangle 2: scalene
Triangle 3: obtuse isosceles

35: Construction

1   Use a protractor to check that all angles in the constructed triangle are 60°.

2   Check by measuring with protractor and ruler that the angles are right angles and that each line is cut in half.

3   Check by measuring with a protractor that each angle is cut in half.

4   Check by measuring with a protractor that each angle is a right angle.

Try it yourself!
If the end points of the line AB are joined to the points where the arcs cross, a rhombus is formed. One diagonal of the rhombus is the line AB; the other is the perpendicular bisector drawn, which is at right angles to the line AB.

36: Perimeter and area

1   20 cm, 21 cm²

2   23 cm, 30 cm²

3   a 40 cm, 79 cm²

    b 38 cm, 76 cm²

    c 40 cm, 88 cm²

4   a 28 cm, 39 cm²

    b 40 cm, 85 cm²

    c 42 cm, 96 cm²

5   a 40 cm, 64 cm²

    b 44 cm, 81 cm²

    c 50 cm, 90 cm²

Try it yourself!
28 cm

37: Circles

1   a radius   b minor arc

    c segment   d circumference

    e diameter   f major sector

    g major arc   h tangent

    i semicircle   j minor sector

    k chord   l segment

2   a 10.05 cm   b 27.02 cm

    c 29.53 cm   d 18.22 cm

3   a 78.54 cm²   b 162.86 cm²

    c 103.87 cm²   d 124.69 cm²

4   a 14.14 cm   b 31.42 cm

    c 37.70 cm

5   a 54.94 cm²   b 21.46 cm²

    c 41.10 cm²

Try it yourself!
1.18 cm

38: Surface area

1   184 cm²

2   142 cm²

3   280 cm²

4   a 358 cm²   b 228 cm²

    c 112 cm²   d 474 cm²

5   5 cm

1 **a** 168 cm³   **b** 112 cm³

  c 210 cm³   **d** 56 cm³

  e 60 cm³   **f** 324 cm³

  g 240 cm³   **h** 100 cm³

2 **a** 188 cm²   **b** 144 cm²

  c 214 cm²   **d** 142 cm²

  e 94 cm²   **f** 306 cm²

  g 236 cm²   **h** 240 cm²

3

Box	Volume (cm³)	Surface area (cm²)
A	60	104
B	64	112
C	216	246
D	210	242
E	72	120
F	252	254

4 **a** 240 cm³, 288 cm²

  b 300 cm³, 360 cm²

  c 54 cm³, 120 cm²

  d 540 cm³, 468 cm²

  e 48 cm³, 108 cm²

  f 60 cm³, 158.8 cm²

5 35 cm³

1 **a** 168 cm³   **b** 240 cm³

  c 324 cm³   **d** 56 cm³

2 **a** 240 cm³   **b** 63 cm³

  c 165 cm³   **d** 300 cm³

3 **a** 60 cm³   **b** 192 cm³

  c 55 cm³

4 **a** 120 cm³   **b** 346.5 cm³

  c 348 cm³

5 **a** 1257 cm³   **b** 2799 cm³

  c 855 cm³   **d** 1140 cm³

Try it yourself!
982 mm³

1 **a** 41°   **b** 35°

  c 94°   **d** 90°

  e 89°

2 **a**   **b**

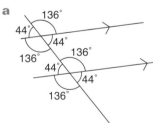

3 $a = 47°$, $b = 133°$, $c = 47°$, $d = 139°$, $e = 41°$

4 $f = 125°$, $g = 55°$, $h = 100°$, $i = 100°$

5 $j = 125°$, $k = 55°$, $l = 100°$, $m = 125°$

6 $n = 51°$, $o = 51°$, $p = 75°$, $q = 105°$, $r = 75°$, $s = 54°$

7 $t = 55°$, $u = 10°$, $v = 115°$

Try it yourself!
72°, 72° and 36° or 36°, 36° and 108°

1 **a** 720° **b** 1440°

  c 540° **d** 1260°

  e 900° **f** 1800°

2 **a** 135° **b** 129°

  c 120° **d** 144°

  e 140° **f** 108°

3 $a = 82°$. The interior angles are 140°, 120°, 98°, 100° and 82°, the corresponding exterior angles are 40°, 60°, 82°, 80° and 98°.

4 167° to nearest degree

5 30

6 20

7 18

8 $x = 61°$. The interior angles are 156°, 135°, 50°, 80°, 119°.

9 $x = 275°$

10 1080°

11 **a** For polygon **i** $x = 20°$. For polygon **ii** $x = 40°$.

  b For polygon **i** the interior angles are 50°, 160°, 160°, 40° and 130°. For polygon **II** the interior angles are 120°, 90°, 160°, 110°, 160° and 80°.

Try it yourself!
$360 - 6x$

1 **a** 1.5 **b** 2.5

  c 3 **d** 2

2 **b** heptagon, **c** square, **d** octagon

3 The coordinates of the images produced are

  a (2, 4), (4, 4), (6, 8), (2, 6)

  b (2, −1), (2, −2), (4, −3), (3, −1)

  c (1, −6), (2, −6), (3, −8), (1, −7)

  d (−3, 2), (−4, 2), (−5, 4), (−3, 3)

  e (−7, −6), (−4, −6), (−1, 0), (−7, −3)

Try it yourself!
A rotation through 90° clockwise

1 14

2 13

3 **a** 3 **b** 4

  c 1, 2, 4, 7, 11, 16, 22

4

1 × 1 squares	1	4	9	16	25
2 × 2 squares	0	1	4	9	16
3 × 3 squares	0	0	1	4	9
4 × 4 squares	0	0	0	1	4
5 × 5 squares	0	0	0	0	1

5

1 × 1 × 1 cubes	1	8	27	64
2 × 2 × 2 cubes	0	1	8	27
3 × 3 × 3 cubes	0	0	1	8
4 × 4 × 4 cubes	0	0	0	1
Total number of cubes	1	9	36	100

6 There are 48 triangles in the pattern.
  25 + 13 + 6 + 3 + 1 = 48

Try it yourself!
No, it is impossible because the angles inside a triangle add to 180°. If there were two obtuse angles (between 90° and 180°), then the angles would have a sum greater than 180°.

45: Coordinates and Pythagoras' theorem

1
  a (3, 3)   b (5, 4)

    c (−2, −3)   d (−2, −4)

    e (−3, 1)   f (1, 2)

    g (3.5, −4)   h (−2, 6.5)

    i (1, 2.5)   j (−3.5, −4.5)

2 Points plotted as a check.

3
  a 7.2 cm   b 10.2 cm

    c 6.8 cm   d 7.7 cm

    e 10.2 cm   f 10.2 cm

4
  a 5   b 4.5

    c 4.5   d 10

    e 7.6

Try it yourself!
A 3 cm, 4 cm, 5 cm and **C** 5 cm, 12 cm, 13 cm

46: Statistics

1 mode = 12, median = 16, mean = 17.9, range = 28

2 mean = 6.44, mode = 6

3 380

4 50

5 6.48

6 99%

7 49

8 30

9 mean = 28.5 (to 1 d.p.), median = 29, mode = 29

Try it yourself!
8.9

47: Graphs and charts (1)

1 a $\frac{128}{240}$ b 192°

2 Girls' preferences:

Flavour	Frequency	Calculation (fraction × 360)	Angle of sector
Cheese and onion	23	$\frac{23}{80} \times 360$	103.5°
Prawn cocktail	13	$\frac{13}{80} \times 360$	58.5°
Ready salted	4	$\frac{4}{80} \times 360$	18°
Salt and vinegar	11	$\frac{11}{80} \times 360$	49.5°
Smoky bacon	21	$\frac{21}{80} \times 360$	94.5°
Other	8	$\frac{8}{80} \times 360$	36°

Boys' preferences:

Flavour	Frequency	Calculation (fraction × 360)	Angle of sector
Cheese and onion	31	$\frac{31}{110} \times 360$	101°
Prawn cocktail	8	$\frac{8}{110} \times 360$	26°
Ready salted	5	$\frac{5}{110} \times 360$	16°
Salt and vinegar	28	$\frac{28}{110} \times 360$	92°
Smoky bacon	21	$\frac{21}{110} \times 360$	69°
Other	17	$\frac{17}{110} \times 360$	56°

3 Check that the pie charts match the angles given above, and that they have a key and title.

4 More girls than boys like prawn cocktail flavour crisps.

  More boys than girls like salt and vinegar flavour crisps.

  More girls than boys like smoky bacon flavour crisps.

  More boys than girls like other flavours of crisps.

Try it yourself!
1280

1   a positive correlation   b zero correlation

    c negative correlation

2   See the scatter graph below.

3   positive correlation

4   See graph

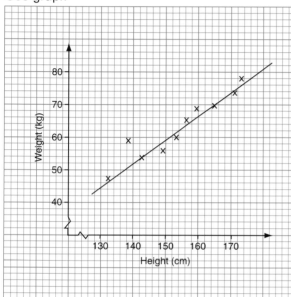

5   a about 152 cm   b about 156 cm

6   a about 55 kg   b about 72 kg

Try it yourself!
Pairs that might show positive correlation:

▶ time spent revising and the mark gained in a test

▶ age of a child and their bedtime

▶ summer temperature and number of ice-creams sold

▶ heights and weights of children of the same age

▶ amount of money spent on advertising and popularity of a product.

1   a $\frac{1}{2}$ b $\frac{1}{6}$

    c $\frac{2}{7}$

2   Fractions equivalent to these are also acceptable.

    a $\frac{5}{26}$ b $\frac{1}{13}$ or $\frac{4}{52}$

    c $\frac{1}{4}$ or $\frac{13}{52}$ d $\frac{3}{6}$ or $\frac{1}{2}$

    e $\frac{2}{6}$ or $\frac{1}{3}$ f 0

3   Fractions equivalent to these are also acceptable.

    a $\frac{1}{10}$ b $\frac{9}{10}$

    c $\frac{4}{10}$ d $\frac{6}{10}$

    e $\frac{3}{10}$ f $\frac{7}{10}$

    g $\frac{4}{10}$ h $\frac{6}{10}$

4   $\frac{3}{8}$ marked on a 0–1 probability scale, e.g. 3 cm from 0 mark on an 8 cm-long scale

5   a $\frac{1}{8}$ b $\frac{1}{4}$

    c $\frac{3}{8}$ d $\frac{3}{8}$

    e $\frac{1}{4}$ f $\frac{7}{8}$

    g $\frac{5}{8}$ h $\frac{3}{4}$

    i $\frac{3}{8}$ j $\frac{1}{8}$

    k $\frac{1}{8}$ l $\frac{1}{2}$

6   3, 4, 2, 1, 2

1   Equivalent fractions are acceptable.

   a $\frac{4}{7}$ **b** $\frac{7}{9}$

   c $\frac{7}{25}$, 0.28, 28%

2   **a**

	Red	Blue	Green
1	$\frac{1}{5}$, 0.2, 20%	$\frac{13}{20}$, 0.65, 65%	$\frac{3}{20}$, 0.15, 15%
2	$\frac{13}{50}$, 0.26, 26%	$\frac{29}{50}$, 0.58, 58%	$\frac{4}{25}$, 0.16, 16%
3	$\frac{1}{4}$, 0.25, 25%	$\frac{63}{100}$, 0.63, 63%	$\frac{3}{25}$, 0.12, 12%

   b set C

3

	Red	Blue	Green
Bag K	9	63	18
Bag L	35	14	21
Bag M	2	26	12
Bag N	27	9	24

4   **a** 46/190, 118/190, 26/190

   b 19, 50, 11

5   The statement is false. It is just as likely that the same numbers will come up as before.

Note to parents

This book is designed to challenge and extend children aged 11–14 in the key Maths topics in the curriculum at Key Stage 3. *Maths Challenge* involves the more complex aspects of Maths in the curriculum and provides opportunities for children to be challenged and extended in their understanding.

The book is designed to be used by children throughout the year. Each double-page spread provides information about the nature of the topic, the key aspects that children are expected to master, and provides opportunities for them to practise and test their own understanding.

By working through the book, your child will encounter the more difficult Mathematics concepts and be encouraged to solve problems and puzzles requiring an advanced level of mathematical thinking.

The Maths curriculum at KS3 and the National Tests

The Key Stage 3 Strategy is designed to make the most of the time between primary school and GCSEs. It provides training for teachers, materials for pupils and advice for everyone involved in making the classroom experience as effective as possible. The Strategy provides a framework for teaching mathematics in Years 7, 8 and 9, identifying the aspects of maths to be taught and the expectations for pupils. The main strands of learning at Key Stage 3 are as follows.

- Using and applying mathematics to solve problems.
- Numbers and the number system.
- Calculations.
- Algebra.
- Shape, space and measures.
- Handling data.

Children at Key Stage 3 who attend state schools in England sit National Tests (also known as SATs) at the age of 14. Children in Wales may take the same tests at 14. All children may also sit optional tests aged 12 and 13 – many schools have chosen to adopt these tests. The results are used by the school to assess each child's level of knowledge and progress in maths, English and science. They also provide guidance for the child's next teacher when he or she is planning the coming year.

This book provides opportunities for children to prepare for these tests, by ensuring that they are challenged in the more complex topics. It is important that this is not a last-minute activity, but forms part of the on-going revision work throughout the year. The children who succeed in maths are those who evaluate their own understanding of each topic as they encounter it and take steps to improve areas of difficulty by further study. This book provides a wide range of opportunities for children to be stretched and to meet the more difficult mathematical problems that they may face in the National Tests.

Levels of attainment

Teachers gain information about your child's progress through testing and on-going teacher assessment. You will be informed each year of your child's level of attainment. Each level is a measure that teachers use to check how much your child knows, understands and can do. National expectations are that by the end of Key Stage 1 pupils achieve at least level 2, by the end of Key Stage 2 level 4 and above, by the end of Key Stage 3 level 5 and above.

How to use this book

Encourage your child to work through the topics in this book and test their understanding by answering the questions and solving the problems and puzzles. It is not necessary to work through the topics in the order that they are given.

Throughout the book are 'Try it yourself!' puzzles which encourage your child to develop more effective thinking skills and provide more complex situations for children to challenge themselves with. These can be tackled independently of the rest of the page and can serve as a revision question when a topic is revisited.

What can parents do to help?

Learning, and especially revision, is best if active. The more effective practice in a topic a child experiences, the more confident he or she will become. The more confident a child is, the more ready they are for challenges and extension work, which leads to greater achievement.

Once a child thinks they have mastered a topic it can help if you offer to be the pupil! Can they teach it to you? If they can teach you something, they really know and understand it! Explaining something to someone else is one of the best ways of consolidating learning. This approach also shows that you are interested in the topics they are learning and are acknowledging and celebrating their progress.

What next?

Once children have worked through the *Challenge* book and are confident with all the topics, they can prepare for the National Tests using the *WHS National Test Practice Papers* books. These contain practice tests to be taken under exam conditions and can help you to assess the level at which your child is working.